Pre-Sentence Investigation Through the First 90 Days in Federal Prison (From Cell 2 Soul)

Scott Brooks Jr.

Published by Scott Brooks Jr., 2023.

PRE-SENTENCE INVESTIGATION THROUGH THE FIRST 90 DAYS IN FEDERAL PRISON (FROM CELL 2 SOUL)

First edition. October 24, 2023.

Copyright © 2023 Scott Brooks Jr..

ISBN: 978-1961868045

Written by Scott Brooks Jr..

Also by Scott Brooks Jr.

Doing Time the Right Way
A Meaningful Life Requires Meaningful Effort

New Fish Companion Series
Pre-Sentence Investigation Through the First 90 Days in Federal Prison (From Cell 2 Soul)
Federal Prison Etiquette (From Cell 2 Soul)

Soul Call Series
A Soul Call from Prison: How Yoga and Taoism Cured My Crises with Cocaine and Christianity
365 Meditations on the Kolbrin

To All the Old Heads Who Showed a New Fish the Ropes

Introduction

This book starts my *New Fish Companion Series*. Each installment will provide relevant and actionable information to help the newly convicted adjust to federal prison. This edition focuses solely on what occurs post-conviction through the first, three-months in custody.

Though my previous books have focused more on spiritual, mental, and physical health, all discussed my experience with incarceration. Take any basic writing course, and the first thing they tell you is to write about what you know. That adage made this series inevitable. After spending twenty-two years, eleven months, and eighteen days in federal custody, you could say I know more than most people selling their expertise to the recently convicted.

I'm not the first to cover this subject. Many people have gotten into prison consultancy in the past few years. Chris Hart and Will Ferrel even made a funny movie about it, but don't worry, none of my advice will encourage you to hit your knees in a toilet stall.

A new bar got set in this industry when word spread that Mossimo Giannulli and Lori Laughlin paid a firm $100,000 to prepare them for the short sentences both served in minimum-security federal camps. I'm not sure how much value you could expect for that whopping sum, but I'm confident I can provide more bang for your buck than those two got.

Today, the top people in prison consulting, drawing the largest fees, seem to be ex-politicians or men and women who once worked for the Federal Bureau of Prisons. These retired Justice Department workers and such may be familiar with life in a penitentiary. They may even be able to offer a little bit of practical advice about life inside, but there is only one way to *know* what doing time is like.

If you face a stretch behind the razor wire, seek insight from someone who has been there. Many retired wardens have gotten into this business which seems almost comical to me. Most wardens spend all day in their offices away from the main compound. They stand mainline during the lunch meal a couple days a week and walk through the cellblocks five or six times a year. Some never do it. The idea that they could help new fish adjust to incarceration is hilarious.

No warden knows what if feels like to be alone in one of the most hostile places on Earth. They've never had to fight the claustrophobia caused a months-long lockdown in an 8' by 12' cell. They've never experienced a "civil" death where even your loved ones begin to think about you in the past tense.

If you face prison, and bought this book, you probably don't think of yourself as a criminal. You may have made a simple mistake or a few poor decisions leading to conviction. Now, you're left facing a scary situation.

You may be educated, maybe even a professional in your field, and while normally functioning at a high level in society, this predicament makes you aware of social skills you desperately lack. Maybe you have doubts you're tough enough to face the coming ordeal.

If so, don't worry. I had a difficult learning curve too. Unlike many convicts, I got arrested during my final semester, as a senior in college. Though I thought of myself as an alpha male before incarceration, I still felt a lot of fear when I first got locked up.

To survive in there, as a twenty-three-year-old, white kid, with little street experience. I had to figure out the unwritten rules pretty fast. I was lucky to meet a few cons in county jail who had done previous federal bits. These "old heads", in prison slang, taught me critical etiquette to avoid trouble. Through them, I learned to cast a small shadow, stay out of the way, and do my own time. I also learned how to operate within the Federal Bureau of Prisons, dealing with staff and filing paperwork when necessary.

I managed to get through twenty-three years with only one incident report (a *shot,* a write up for breaking prison rules.) I was able to walk away from most confrontations and only got into a handful of fistfights. My worst experience involved an eighty-man brawl where my *car* (a group of homies from the same geographical region) were outnumbered three to one. The incident left me injured, but I didn't need hospitalization and recovered completely in about a month.

This series culls its information from some of the advice I give clients in my private consulting business. I wrote these books as reference guides to those who have purchased my services, as well as to provide information to the many cons who aren't able to hire my company. I also hope my writing reassures worried family members by answering their questions, easing their anxiety, and providing an example of how, with the right attitude, incarceration, can be turned into a transformational experience.

My inspiration for this series came after researching other prison-consulting firms. Most offer a shallow approach at best, and the worst seem more like scam artists, than true professionals offering real value to clients. You would be surprised by how many of these so called "experts" have never spent a day inside a federal facility or were brief tourists at a minimum-security camp.

In answer to this lack, I created a comprehensive system addressing every question first-time offenders need answered including many they wouldn't even know to ask. You see, every "old head" con is a prison consultant. New fish climb off the weekly buses looking dazed, scared, and confused. Any old timer with a little compassion in his heart usually picks one of these lost souls to show the ropes to, explain the rules, and teach them how to do time. I spent many years practicing this profession even before I got out and started my company.

To do a thorough job showing *you* the ropes required me to create a Five Part Strategy. The resulting system fills the seven installments in my *New Fish Companion Series*. This book, coincides with Part I in my Five Step Strategy. Here's a look at what each step offers:

Part I: Post Conviction through the First 90 Days in Custody

This will be the most stressful time, with the most stuff going on for first-time offenders. I'll cover the post-conviction process, including the Presentence Investigation with a federal probation officer. After that, I'll explain what to expect during the first, three months in prison. I'll help you avoid common mistakes new fish make and show you how to get as comfortable as the experience allows in as short an amount of time as possible. Above all, I'll teach you how to cast a small shadow and not step on toes unintentionally.

Part II: Prison Etiquette

In every social interaction with people, there are unwritten rules to learn and social skills to develop, prison is no different. In the free world, rude behavior, breaking your word, telling a lie, or damaging the property of others might cost you a friend or the chance at a second date. At worst, you'll get shunned by a group of peers. In prison, the consequences can be more severe.

This Part covers the basics about fitting in, learning how to avoid tension, conflict de-escalation, and making safety a priority while serving time.

Part III: Learning How the Federal Bureau of Prisons Works

While inmates lose many rights when they go into custody, they don't lose all of them. While many prisoners feel overwhelmed by the prevailing sense of helplessness inside, they aren't powerless. This book teaches the recently convicted to use the FBOP's rules, regulations, and procedures to protect themselves, and take advantage of the few privileges available to convicts.

Part IV: Doing Time the Right Way

Since prison can be one of the most stressful experiences a human can go through, this part teaches convicts how to cope with life behind the razor wire. It draws on techniques that helped me survive so long in federal prison. To cover this properly, this part required three volumes:

Volume 1: Making Mental Health a Priority

This volume teaches effective techniques to combat the mental stress incarceration creates. It also offers advice to help avoid the typical mistakes convicts make regarding idle hours, wasted time, dealing with long-distance relationships, and preparing for release. Most importantly, it gives detailed instructions for creating proactive routines to combat the feeling that your life is being wasted while you serve time.

Volume 2: Making Physical Health a Priority.

This one focuses on helping an inmate stay as healthy as possible while he or she serves time. It offers creative routines that take into consideration the limited equipment available inside of a federal facility. Armed with this knowledge, a convict can leave prison young and vibrant with some good years still ahead.

Volume III: Making Spiritual Health a Priority

Volume 3 focuses on spiritual health. I consider it the most important in the entire *New Fish Companion Series*. I couldn't have gotten through all that time without a meditation practice. It helped me cope with guilt. It helped me become a better man.

In it, I teach the ways I found meaning and purpose while doing all that time. It speaks to the religiously-minded and agnostic equally. A digital copy can be downloaded for free from my website: fromcell2soul.com.

Part V: A Fresh Start: Reentry Options Available Upon Release from Federal Prison

Aside from the first months in custody, the most stressful time for many inmates comes when they near release. Though every person in custody spends many moments dreaming about the day he or she gets to leave, it can be an anxiety-filled experience when it finally arrives. This Part explains home confinement, halfway-house placement, rules, and relocations, as well as federal probation. It includes reentry prep and covers all the resources available to help ex-cons get back on their feet. It also covers special physical and mental health considerations unique to the recently released and potential solutions to these issues.

This may come as a surprise, but with the right mindset, and a little guidance, prison ain't all bad. Sure, inmates dream about their release every day in there, but incarceration provides leisure time like few other life experiences. With the wrong outlook, all those idle years can drive a person crazy, but with an optimistic attitude *and* a plan, a felon can change his or her life for the better, gain skills, learn interesting subjects, get in great physical shape, pick up a talent or hobby, and most importantly, develop inner fortitude by learning how to rise above circumstances and face adversity with the correct approach.

Table of Contents

Part One: Special Considerations When Granted a Federal Bond

A. Pre-Trial Release

Given a choice, almost everyone indicted by the federal government would choose pre-trial release over getting trapped in a county jail or federal detention center while waiting for things to play out. Unfortunately, according to Department of Justice statistics, only 32% of newly indicted men and women are given this opportunity after their arrests. Though it happens rarely, a federal judge can grant release on personal recognizance, conditional release, temporary detention, or detention prior to trial.

Usually, if the person faces more than ten years of imprisonment, committed an act of terrorism, trafficked humans, or hurt a minor, they will not receive pre-trial release. If you want to know your eligibility, this would be a matter best discussed with your attorney. Although I can't offer legal advice, I *will* try to provide some insights here that your lawyer may or may not have covered with you.

1. Home Inspection

The main task will be preparing your residence for an inspection by a federal probation officer. The PO should explain the rules beforehand, but I'll go over the pertinent ones. First, if the judge grants a bond, expect certain conditions, like: Pre-trial supervision by a federal probation officer, drug testing, mental health treatment, travel restrictions, the surrender of all travel documents, electronic monitoring, or a curfew, and all are used to ensure you appear in court.

Before your home inspection, clear your home of all weapons. If your spouse or relatives own firearms, they will need to store them at another location or buy a gun safe with a key lock, not a combination lock. You cannot have access to the key.

Obviously, all drugs need to be removed as well, along with any other contraband that could cause new charges to be filed. That includes marijuana and all other hemp products. It doesn't matter if you live in a legal state or that you can buy Delta 8 in all fifty. Federal law still prohibits it, and you will violate your bond if you piss dirty for THC or CBD.

Depending on your alleged crime, criminal history, and confessed proclivities, you may not be allowed to drink or possess internet access. The judge has lots of leeway. He can get creative with his conditions.

B. Self-Surrendering

Even if you are granted pre-trial release, you may be taken into custody after conviction or after taking a plea. This is something to discuss with your attorney. If so, you'll sit in county jail or a Federal Holding Center until you get sentenced. After receiving your punishment, you'll be transferred to FBOP custody, within a few months.

Self-Surrendering is a special privilege given to certain inmates. Usually, recipients accepted responsibility for their crime by pleading guilty. Some get to turn themselves in at their assigned prison, because they cooperated with the federal government. Some face minor charges and short sentences, if any time at all. Famous people often get this special treatment too. It might not seem fair, but it's definitely true.

1. What You Can Bring

Rules vary from prison to prison, especially as you go up in custody-level, but some minimum-security camps will allow you to bring a few items that the higher-securities will ban. You can check your designated prison's website for details. Unfortunately, that data often is outdated. You can try calling the prison, but good luck with finding a helpful FBOP official.

In general, Federal Bureau of Prisons' regulations prohibit inmates from possessing any item worth more than $100. Every facility will allow you to bring in prescription eyeglasses. Just make sure the frames don't contain precious metals. Most places will let you have an extra pair and even contacts with cleaning solution, but obtaining replacement contacts or fluid may be a problem. Other medical devices, like hearing aids, prosthetics, canes, and such, will be allowed in too.

As far as jewelry, they will allow you to keep a simple wedding band. Ladies won't be allowed to wear expensive engagement rings inside though. It wouldn't be smart to have something like that in a prison even if it were allowed. My first rule for survival in there is:

Cast a Small Shadow

Don't make yourself a target for theft or anything else. Don't flaunt wealth, especially if you're loaded. Don't brag. Don't bling.

Religious medallions, like a cross, and holy books can be brought from home or purchased through the prison's chaplain. The $100 rule applies here too. Wear it on a semi-precious chain, cotton cord, or leather thong. Just be aware that if you put the medallion on something extra strong, you might give a potential enemy a handle to choke you by in an altercation. Think *Mortal Kombat*, "Get over here!"

If you keep the $100 rule in mind, you might be able to keep a cheap Timex watch (or G Shock), but I would bring a receipt to be sure. Some complexes might allow you to keep your shoes, but that's a gamble. Just make sure they only sport black, white, and/or grey. The FBOP doesn't want to give any gang a chance to exhibit its colors (e.g., Bloods/Red, CRIPS/Blue, Surreños/Blue/Black/Brown...etc.), and you don't want the homies to think you are flying their flag.

"Hey vato! You down with tha Latin Kings or what, ese'?"

Honestly, regarding shoes and watches, you might be better off getting them at the prison commissary. You can have a friend or family member send you money, quickly.

They can put money on your account with Western Union. The money clears within two hours.

Western Union Quick Collect

This only takes a couple hours for the money to hit the inmate's account.
Call 1-800-325-6000 or www.westernunion.com[1]
Must Provide:

1. Valid Eight Digit Register Number without spaces or dashes
2. Inmate's name entered on the *Attention* line
3. Code City: FBOP, DC
4. The Western Union app now has a special feature to simplify sending money to prisoners

US Postal Services

---

1.   http://www.westernunion.com

Send a US Postal Money order with the inmate's name and registration number to:

Federal Bureau of Prisons

Committed Inmate's Name

Reg. # 99999-999

PO BOX 474701

Des Moines, Iowa 50947-0001

Use this address no matter where the inmate is housed in the system.

US Postal Money Orders get deposited immediately. Non-government money orders will be accepted but take fifteen days to clear. Personal checks will be refused.

DO NOT send money to the prison where the inmate is housed

Most prisons allow a *Fish Draw*. Inmates are assigned a particular day of the week to shop, but they make exceptions for first-time shoppers. If your facility does this, you may be able to go to commissary the day you arrive. If not, you probably will be able to purchase items on the next week day. I'll cover all the stuff you'll need to buy later.

2. Potential Issues with Self-Surrendering

a. False Assumptions

If you do self-surrender, you might face an issue with other inmates making assumptions about you. The worst conclusion they might jump to is that you cooperated with the government to get the special treatment. Some might call you a rat after they learn how you arrived at the prison. It may be an unfair, even an untrue, claim, but it still may happen.

Unfortunately, you won't be able to keep self-surrendering a secret. Other inmates work at Receiving and Discharge (R and D). Everyone will know your circumstances the day you arrive.

If you self-surrender at a camp, it won't matter. It won't matter even if did testify for a time cut. Guys have very short sentences, are rats themselves, or are "old heads" at the end of very long sentences. No one will pose a danger to you. In fact, anyone with a violent conviction, or with a non-violent conviction who seriously injured another prisoner while incarcerated, will never go to a camp.

Sex offenders are not allowed at camps either. There are a bunch at the low-security prisons though, but most are child molesters. Low facilities do not have a tremendous amount of violence either. Guys might talk down to you if they think you got a 5K(1) or a Rule 35(b) sentence reduction, because you self-surrendered. You might get banned from the TV rooms, but they won't harm you as long as you show them respect.

If you self-surrender at a medium, assumptions may be made a little more quickly, because few inmates in medium custody are allowed this perk. Still, it depends on which complex you have to report at. Some mediums are as soft as lows and camps. Some are considered "protective-custody" yards. Others check paperwork and beat up rats, sex offenders, and inmates who steal from other prisoners.

If you don't have sex charges, and you didn't testify against anyone, you won't start out with any enemies or problems. If you self-surrender under these circumstances, advertise you have nothing to hide. Your homies will show you how to provide paperwork (proof you didn't cooperate), if you want to play along, but this step is becoming less necessary.

Contraband smart phones make keeping secrets impossible, and most facilities have them now. Someone in every cellblock has a *Pacer* account for tracking court records. I'll get into how to handle this in more detail later.

b. County Benefits

There are other disadvantages to self-surrendering. First, jail time credit will come off your federal sentence unless you have issues with state charges coinciding with the federal ones. (Discuss specifics about jail credit with your attorney.) If you have to spend six months in county or a Federal Detention Center, you'll be that much closer to release when you transfer to prison.

Anyone who has had to endure county jail would tell you it sucks, but after spending many months doing hard time like that, the federal-prison experience doesn't seem so bad in comparison. It definitely creates a perspective of gratitude for the few amenities available at a federal facility like fresh air, green grass, and numerous programs that help pass the time. By comparison, if you self-surrender, you'll have a completely different mind-set when you enter the front gate.

Most importantly, county jail allows first-timers to start learning the ropes in a more forgiving environment. Plus, repeat offenders love to pass time in the boring county-jail setting by teaching new fish some of the same information my prison consulting firm offers clients, but reading this book series also will prepare the recently convicted for their coming ordeal.

Part Two: Pre-Sentence Investigation

A. Purpose

This is an interview conducted by a federal probation officer soon after conviction. The primary purpose is to present the sentencing judge with a guideline range for punishment. Sentencing won't take place until after your PO has completed the Pre-Sentence Report (PSR).

B. RDAP Eligibility

The Residential Drug Abuse Program is a nine-month course where participants live in a special cellblock together. Eligible inmates receive a twelve-month sentence reduction upon successful completion. Recipients cannot have a violent charge, a non-violent gun charge, or a sex case greater than simple possession of illegal pornography. In addition, anyone with a sentence shorter than thirty-six months may *not* have sufficient time to enroll and complete the process fast enough to earn the full year reduction.

Other criteria need to be met besides the restriction based on current conviction. First, criminal history is taken into consideration. Any previous violent charge less than ten years in the past also disqualifies inmates for the cut. The ten-year timeline doesn't start until the punishment ended for the past offenses.

The criteria most pertinent to the Pre-Sentence Investigation concerns documenting past drug abuse. If the PSR doesn't indicate you've battled problems with narcotics or alcohol, you won't be entitled to earn the one-year sentence reduction, even if you meet all other criteria. This interview will be the only opportunity to confess a problem with drugs or alcohol. If you choose to hide your problem due to embarrassment, you will be allowed to enroll in the program at the prison. You can take the course, but you won't earn the time cut.

If you are given pre-trial release, if would be best to demonstrate your sincerity in trying to fix this issue by seeking permission to go to rehab, AA, or NA while you await trial. This is also the best way to document the existence of a substance abuse issue. If you were denied bail, see if the county jail offers drug classes or AA meetings. Seek help while you await the resolution of your case and inform your lawyer, PO, and judge of your efforts.

If you have drug charges, it will be much easier to establish a history of addiction, but it really doesn't matter if you weren't a dealer or robbed bank to support a habit. The probation officer is obligated to help you get the rehabilitation you need no matter your charges.

My buddy had a non-violent drug conviction. He didn't have any priors and his lack of criminal history entitled him to do his time at a minimum-security camp. When he met with his probation officer, he denied a past drug addiction. He did this partly from embarrassment, partly because he got clean on his own waiting for trial, and partly because he thought a confession of this nature would lead to intense drug testing on probation after his release.

The most important effect his reluctance brought was to guarantee he stayed in federal prison a year longer than he should have. When he got to his assigned camp, he went to the psychiatric department and confessed his addiction. They told him he was welcome to sign up for RDAP, but he would not earn the year time cut for it.

White-collar criminals who confess a drug or alcohol problem during the interview will be eligible for the year off. It applies to fraud, embezzlement, bank robbery using a note (no weapon), child pornography (possession only, no touch cases), and all the other non-violent crimes are all eligible.

On the other hand, if you have a violent charge, sex crime, or certain non-violent gun possession convictions (Ask your lawyer about eligibility), you can't earn the year no mater what you claim at your interview. If you honestly need treatment, you can take RDAP, NRDAP (The Non-Residential Drug Abuse Program), or the forty-hour drug program. The last one will be court mandated, if you have a drug conviction. You will be forced to take the forty-hour one, or you will be placed on maintenance pay, lose First-Step Time Credits, and be denied halfway-house placement.

As a final thought, an admission about prior drug use will affect custody points, as you'll see in the next section. Also, if your PSR states you battled addiction, you may face more intense drug screening on federal probation after your release.

C. The Initial Custody Classification

1. How it relates to Your Assigned Prison

Probably your biggest worry after conviction, besides how long your sentence will be, will concern the prison the Bureau chooses for you. The first worry has to do with location. Unfortunately, many states do not have any federal prisons. Others don't have all custody levels. For example, South Carolina has four mediums and four camps but no pens or lows.

The First Step Act of 2018 created a requirement for the FBOP to house every inmate within five-hundred "driving" miles of their release address. This isn't possible for all inmates, especially those coming from the many Mid-Western States without any federal facilities at all. Also, this provision becomes null and void if a security issue is involved, like the convict is a violent, trouble maker or requires protective custody.

The first purpose of the Pre-Sentence Investigation is to research and define the sentencing guidelines the judge will be bound by when imposing punishment. The guidelines determine sentence length based on the severity of convicted offenses defined by law. Then, using factors, like the crime's seriousness, time imposed, and other details, custody classification gets determined. This designation will weigh heavily on the minds of new convicts. It's important, because the designation determines whether a prisoner goes to a penitentiary, a medium FCI, a low security, or a minimum, out-custody, camp.

2. How to Tabulate Custody Points

I'm going to explain the custody classification process, so you can add up your own score. This will allow you to double check your probation officer's tally. It is important to get it right, because it only takes a few points to move you from one custody level to another. If this seems too complicated, tabulating custody points is one of the many things we do for clients at *From Cell 2 Soul Federal Prison Consulting.*

The following information can be found in the *Federal Bureau of Prisons' Program Statement PS 5100.08.*

Here are the factors considered which determine whether you start out at a camp, low, medium, or penitentiary: age, education level, drug/alcohol abuse history, mental/psychological stability, responsibility demonstrated (Did you accept a plea?), family/community ties, and violence or other safety factors.

I. Quick Shortcut for Prison Designation

I'll get into how points get tallied in a second, but we can weed out a few people first. You have to have a sentence shorter than ten years (or less than then years remaining on your sentence) to go to a minimum-security camp. Also, sex offenders and violent convicts are prohibited from camps no matter how short the sentence.

To go to a low security, you have to have less than twenty years left till release. Lows allow convicts with all crimes as long as they meet the sentence length requirement and have fifteen or less custody points. Mediums and Highs have all sentence lengths, even lifers. Custody points determine which one the BOP sends a new convict.

II. The Formal Calculation Procedure

1. Prior Calculation:

For the initial classification, if this is your first conviction, start with *zero* points. Otherwise, add *three* points for each prior sentence over a year in length. Add *two* points for each prior sentence where you served more than sixty days. Add *one* point for each prior conviction resulting in less than sixty days.

Add your tally here: _____

2. Age Calculation:

Because younger inmates usually cause the most trouble inside, add *zero* points, if you are fifty-five or older. Add *two* points if aged between thirty-six and fifty-four. Add *four* points, if aged between twenty-five and thirty-five. Add *eight* points, if you're a youngster aged twenty-four or less. (This rating forces most kids to start out at a medium or higher and work their way down.)

(Age Calculation) _____ + (Prior Calculation) _____ = _____

3. Education Tabulation

A college degree doesn't help here, but if you have a high school diploma or GED, add zero points to your tally. Without a diploma, you need to add *two* points. If you fall under the latter category, you will be forced to take a GED class at your designated prison. As soon as classes start, you can subtract *one* point. Unfortunately, your unit team probably will make you wait eighteen months to update the point change in your file.

You might want to show your probation officer a diploma, even one from college, during the Pre-Sentence interview (for those on Pre-Trial release). This will guarantee your file has the correct information. Otherwise, you might get forced to take GED classes or be denied vocational training or other programs until your old high school sends transcripts to the prison. I've seen it happen before. It could complicate things for First Step Eligible inmates trying to program their way out of prison a year early.

Add: (Education Calculation) _____ + (Previous Total) ____ = _____

4. Voluntary Surrender

If you are allowed to self-surrender at your designated prison, subtract three points from the total.

(Total from 3) _____ -3(If Applicable) =_____

5. Detainer Calculation

If you caught a state case with your federal bit, your custody points will be affected. If the state sentence is consecutive (meaning it starts after completion of the federal sentence), it is concurrent (running with the fed bit) but is longer in duration, or the detainer is based on unresolved (pending) charges, you may not be allowed to go to a fenceless, minimum-security camp, because the BOP feels the temptation for you to escape might be too strong.

No detainers, add *zero* points. For a low grade, add *one*. For a medium, add *three*. For a high, add *five*. For the greatest, add *seven* points. Most of the time, detainers add *three, five,* or *seven* points depending on seriousness.

(Total from 4) _____+ (Detainer Calculation) _____=_____

6. Drug or Alcohol Abuse Calculation

If you have never abused either, or it has been longer than five years, add *zero* points. If it has been less than five years, add *one* point. This will be determined by what you tell the probation officer during your interview. You may be tempted to deny a problem to avoid the point, and avoid more stringent drug testing on probation after release, but this would not be wise.

To be eligible for the Residential Drug Abuse Program (RDAP), and a year off your sentence, you have to admit to a drug or alcohol problem during the interview. You can't deny it then and "remember" your addiction later.

(Total from 5) _____+ (Abuse Calculation) _____=_____

7. History of Violence

This includes current conviction, past convictions, and occurrences while in Bureau of Prisons' custody. This one requires a chart, but first, if you have no history of violence, add *zero* points.

>15 years 10-15 years 5-10 years <5 years

Minor 1 1 3 5

Serious 2 4 6 7

(A fistfight is minor. Stomping an unconscious man is serious.)

(Total from 6) _____ + (Violence Calculation) _____= _____

8. Custody Level Chart

Look up your total below:

Security Level Custody Level Male Female

Minimum Out (No Fence) 0-11 Points 0-15 Points

Low In (Behind Razor Wire) 12-15 16-30

Medium In 16-23 (No Mediums)

High Maximum (Walls and Gun 24+ 31+
Towers)

Administrative (All Levels: hospitals, detention centers, SHUS, SMUS, and holdovers)

9. Public Safety Factors

Unfortunately, the Bureau has other ways to prevent inmates from going down in custody. A *Public-Safety Factor* (PSF) can be tacked on in addition to the points accrued for violence. A Public Safety Factor guarantees you will never go to a camp. For example, I had eight points for my final seven years in prison, but my Public Safety Factor, added for a 924(C)-gun charge, kept me from ever transferring to a camp.

The following seven crimes and conditions will earn you a *Public-Safety Factor* designation and guarantee you'll never see a camp no matter your sentence, custody points, programming, or level of remorse.

- Sentence Length: Any sentence over twenty years must be served at a pen or medium. Once you get twenty years till release, you may be able to go to a low, depending on points. You have to be under ten years to go to a camp. This safety factor isn't permanent unless you have a life sentence.
- Disruptive Group: You are a documented member of a gang, terror organization, or hate group.
- Violence: This safety factor may be removed after a number of years with good behavior and programming, but there is no guarantee. You can ask your case manager to file a Form 409 to remove it, but don't hold your breath. I had some tell me they never do this regardless of the situation, and the decision is up to staff's discretion.
- Serious Escape: A minor escape would be walking off a camp compound. A serious one would require busting out of a facility or overpowering a guard while in transit.
- Sex Offense: The FBOP will not risk putting a child molester at a camp they could walk away from and hurt another minor. Sex assaults against staff or other inmates will bring a PSF as well. Rapes against adults count too.
- Deportable Alien: If you will be sent back to your home country when your sentence ends, you can't go to a camp. Talk to your lawyer about a Treaty Transfer, if your country has a more lenient legal system than

the United States. You could potentially, *but doubtfully*, go home to serve your time.

- Serious Telephone Abuse: Making threats. Ordering an attack. Running a criminal enterprise from prison. Any of this will keep you from ever making it to minimum security.

III. Reducing Custody Points

a. Conduct in Custody

Every eighteen months, your unit team is supposed to recalibrate your points. This is a major aggravation point with inmates who have to contend with lazy case managers who look for any excuse to slow walk inmates and avoid work, but you aren't completely helpless.

You have control over a few elements. First, you can take the programs, classes, and courses the prison offers. Second, you can stay out of trouble. Eighteen-months of clear conduct and programming both lower custody points a little. You also lose two points when you turn thirty-six and another two when you turn fifty-five.

b. Resolving Detainers

You also lose points by getting detainers resolved. I had a seven-point detainer for pending state charges. For fifteen years, it prevented me going to a low-security prison. I was stuck at a medium-high until I got the charges dismissed.

I made the charges go away by filing a speedy trial request. Because I had such a lengthy federal sentence, I didn't think a county in North Carolina would waste the money to drag me back from Kansas and put me on trial. Federal law under the *Inter-State Agreements on Detainers* allowed me to do this. You can use it on any pending state charges everywhere but Mississippi and Louisianna.

I went to Receiving and Discharge (R and D) at my prison and told them what I wanted. They filed the necessary paperwork. Afterwards, the BOP informed the county in NC, they had 180 days to put me on trial. At the time, I was more than a thousand miles away at USP Leavenworth. The state declined to come and get me.

I still had more work to do though. After the six months expired, I had to get my lawyer to file a motion to dismiss the charges in state court, but given the circumstances, the judge had no choice except granting my request. A few months after the dismissal, I got my points reduced and received a transfer to a low-security prison.

You need to understand the risk you'll be taking if you do this. Your state might call your bluff and prosecute you. You could end up with more time added to the end of your federal sentence.

Usually, the chances a state will drop charges on their own increases the longer you wait. They lose track of witnesses. Prosecutors familiar with your case leave the office, but if the charges are petty, like driving on a suspended license or a DUI, you might want to roll the dice.

Also, IADs only apply to detainers. If you have a warrant pending, but not lodged with the Federal Bureau of Prisons, this strategy won't work. The good news is that warrants don't affect custody points, but they will prevent an inmate going to a halfway house a year early or receiving the year off after completion of RDAP. If the charges are minor, write the state prosecutor and offer to plead guilty, if he or she will run the time concurrently with your federal sentence. It sometimes works.

Ultimately, it would be best to discuss all these issues with your attorney. Get his or her expertise on this matter, and opinion on how risky the action would be in your particular circumstance, before making a final decision. You do not need counsel to file an IAD. The FBOP will do all the paperwork for you, but they won't file a motion to dismiss on your behalf.

D. PSR's Relevance to Safety

The *Pre-Sentence Report (PSR)* is a published document resulting from the Pre-Sentence Investigation. It contains every detail concerning the convicted crimes. Some read like a book. The probation officer assembles this information from the compiled evidence in the case and the info provided in the interview by the convict.

1. Separatees

The PSR details whether the convict cooperated with the government in any way. For this reason, the PSR is used to establish *separatees*. Separatees are filed against anyone who might be a threat to the inmate.

Other convicts who he testified against usually top the list, but prisoners can file separatees against any con who has threatened or harmed them while in custody. Separatees prevent inmates from being housed at the same facility together. For safety's sake, these details get worked out immediately after a guilty verdict or plea.

Even if you didn't testify against anyone, you may still be affected by separatees. My trial lasted two weeks. Every person who took the stand against me and my codefendants filed separatees on us. I didn't even know over half of the witnesses.

They only offered testimony against the others, but their separatees still affected me. Although from North Carolina, those restrictions caused me to be housed in West Virginia. Since NC only has the Butner complex, and a couple of the witnesses were designated to those prisons near Raleigh, I ended up at FCI-Beckley.

Prosecutors will file separatees for any victims in your case too. It doesn't matter whether they were threatened, physically harmed, scammed, or robbed. Since those people don't face incarceration, this won't affect your assigned prison. Instead, it can cause problems with halfway house placement.

Federal inmates can serve up to one year of their sentence in a Residential Reentry Work Program. This helps cons find jobs, save money, and readjust to freedom in small increments to decrease the probability of recidivism, but prisoners cannot go to a Federal Halfway House within 100 miles of the home address of anyone who filed a separatee against them, unless special approval has been made. This applies to victims and cooperating government witnesses who have been released from, or completely avoided, prison.

2. Checking Paperwork

Since the PSR reveals whether an inmate cooperated, other convicts want to get their hands on these documents to find out who the rats are at their facilities. PSRs also reveal every detail of a defendant's case. These documents expose heinous acts that other inmates consider unacceptable. Since PSRs contain criminal histories too, they will expose anyone who testified on a past case, even if not on the current one. They also could out someone who hurt a child years earlier but not on the conviction they currently serving.

When I entered FBOP custody in 2001, the cellblock's counselor would provide a PSR copy anytime an inmate asked. As soon as I entered the housing unit at my first prison, several cons in my car (white men from the same geographical region as myself) approached me, and told me to go get my PSR. They didn't threaten me overtly, but it went unspoken that I was going to have trouble if I didn't do it. Since my paperwork was "clean", I had no problem showing it to them, and I had no further issues concerning it afterwards.

If I had refused, they would have told me to *check in*. They would have tried to force me to approach the nearest guard and request protective custody. If I had refused that, they would have attacked me, and I would have ended up in PC anyway. On more than one occasion, I've seen a rat, with nasty fists, actually beat up the multiple attackers trying to jump him, but even though he won the fight, he went to PC and later got shipped to another prison. Convicts call this process of checking-in rats, "cleaning the yard."

Several years back, the federal government passed a law that banned PSRs from the list of approved inmate property. If you need to see yours in order to file legal work, your counselor will allow you to view it in his or her office, but you won't be able to take it with you. Also, the legislation made it a crime for an inmate to request to see another prisoner's PSR. The maximum penalty for it carries a five-year sentence added to the time the inmate is already serving.

These days, Receiving and Discharge will confiscate almost all the paperwork you don't hide well when you transfer between prisons. It really doesn't matter anyway. PSRs aren't required to expose confidential information anymore. Almost every facility has contraband smart phones. Someone will look you up shortly after arriving at a new prison.

At USP Leavenworth, a staff member who hated sex offenders would look up every new arrival. The guard then would let a gang member read the court documents on his computer. Within a couple hours, the child molester would be on the ground unconscious, waiting for a guard to find him and call for an ambulance.

I remember one inmate there who had a federal gun charge. Technically, he had *good paperwork*, but no one had seen his PSR because of the new law. He had only shown his *Judgement and Conviction* papers listing his current fed charges. He managed to skate for a few years until a guard checked his record. The prisoner had kidnapped a girl in Tennessee. The sex charges were all *state* charges. He got the *federal* gun charge for shooting at a police helicopter chasing him and the girl through the woods. Once the truth was discovered, he got checked-in immediately.

Because guards have exposed inmates at many prisons, the administration recently restricted lower-level employees from having access to sensitive information. Counselors and case managers can pull up PSRs on their computers, but regular correctional officers only have access to sufficient info pertinent to their safety. New changes like these constantly go into effect to protect vulnerable inmates from harm.

If you're going to a low or camp, it won't matter what skeletons you have in the closet. Serious violence seldom happens at either. Even many mediums these days are pretty soft. Guys there might hate rats and chomos, but few people want to do anything that might bring about new street charges. Things are different at penitentiaries where you have many men doing life and could care less about more time added to their sentences.

Part III: Sentencing

A. A Prison Consultant's Take on the Experience

1. The Bad News

Your attorney will cover potential sentences with you in detail. Honestly, most federal lawyers, even those raking in hefty retainers, don't do much more than point at the sentencing guidelines and tell you what you'll get for pleading out versus the added time you'll face if you go to trial.

Fewer than 1% of federal criminal defendants were acquitted in 2020. 89.4% of defendants took a plea deal. Considering those statistics, and the 100% guarantee you'll be punished much more severely for exercising your Sixth Amendment right to go to trial, these days many federal defense lawyers serve the prosecution more than they do their own clients.

Conspiracy law makes convictions too easy. They need no evidence other than a convicted co-conspirator testifying for a time cut to get a guilty verdict. For this reason, the only option defense attorneys present, other than accepting the first and only offer from an assistant US Attorney, is to become a government witness.

As jaded as that sounds, if you haven't learned the truth in my words yet, you soon will. I am unqualified to offer you any advice that may net you a shorter sentence, and like I already said, when it comes down to it, even the best attorney in the country can't help much either. My lawyer and both of my codefendants' lawyers tried to scare me into accepting a thirty-year deal.

They terrified my mom and dad with tales of the life sentence I would get if I went to trial. At the time, thirty years seemed like my entire life anyway. So, I refused. I got lucky and beat a couple of the charges at trial. I ended up twenty-six years and ten months. So, *not so lucky*, but it could have been worse. Plus, I didn't testify against anyone.

What I've learned through the years is that my example is an anomaly. Most guys who opted to go my route ended up worse by decades. Some got life sentences with non-violent drug crimes when a plea of guilty would have netted them an out date. Obama fixed a few of these cases with his clemency program, and Trump's *First Step Act* helped a few more, but not nearly enough.

Cooperating is about the only way to guarantee a reduction in sentence length, but doing that brings a bunch of other potential consequences, like retaliation, guilt, and extra problems in prison. Throughout my twenty-three years in federal custody, I remember many stories about rats who were murdered within days of their release. A few got killed while they were still housed in a federal halfway house.

Also, some judges refuse to help rats in a substantial way. They have final say over these type agreements. Plus, prosecutors break their promises in these deals, or at least overpromise and not deliver as much as originally agreed. A snitch in my case got a four-month time reduction for putting a meth case on an entire chapter of Hell's Angels. He should probably trade his Harley for a rice rocket and move to Japan when he gets out.

2. The Good News

Enough with the doom and gloom. Let me add a glimmer of hope to the negative experience you're facing. First, the sentencing commission made an across the board two-point reduction for all drugs in 2014. With the exception of fentanyl and heroin, narcotics charges don't carry as much time as they did when I got arrested. In 2010, the disparity between crack and powder cocaine charges decreased from 100:1 to 18:1, and chances are good that they might be equal in the near future. In addition, new court decisions, like Johnson, for gun possession cases, constantly reduce sentences, and sometimes provide guys who've been down a while a chance to get back in court. My co-defendant gave back a life sentence when he got back in court after serving two-decades.

If the above examples don't make you feel like jumping and clacking your heels together, you may be eligible to earn two, time cuts. The first has been around a while, but completion of the nine-month Residential Drug Abuse Program (RDAP) allows some prisoners to earn a year off their sentences. The second, brought about with the First Step Act's passage, has stricter qualifications than RDAP, but can help those eligible to earn another year for programming. Besides a potential twenty-four months off your bit, you could earn up to twelve months in a halfway house or on home confinement. So, things may not be quite as bad as they seem.

B. Problems with Other Charges

1. Concurrent Time

If you also face unresolved state charges, or if you have already been sentenced to state time, ask your lawyer to request your federal time be run concurrent with the other punishment. Judges have discretion in this area, and a favorable ruling could get you out much sooner.

If you have pending state charges after your federal sentence, ask your lawyer to call the state, assistant district attorney. Tell your legal counsel to inform the state prosecutor about the federal sentence. Explain that you are willing to plead guilty (depending on how serious the crime and what your attorney thinks) to the state case, as long as the time is run concurrent with the federal sentence.

Sometimes, they will just drop the charges. Trials can be very expensive, and county, district attorneys have to be more budget conscious than US Attorneys. For instance, while under federal indictment, I had a pending first-degree, murder charge in North Carolina. After my 322-month, federal sentence was imposed, the prosecutor in NC called my lawyer, told him he thought I got railroaded in the fed case, and immediately dropped all state charges. He also knew I wasn't in the room when the man got killed, and the killer had already received life plus ten in his federal case.

2. Jail Credit

If you were refused bail, ask that your fed time start at the date of your arrest. Usually, this is automatic, but sometimes confusion results when local authorities take you into custody first and the feds pick up the case later. If there is any mix-up regarding this when you enter FBOP custody, staff almost always interpret the situation in a way that hurts you. Your judge ruling on it in a positive way at sentencing is the best way to handle the problem.

My buddy spent three years in county jail with pending robbery charges on the state level. Due to his record, he was looking at a potential life sentence, if the state tried him, but after thirty-six months, the state dropped all charges when the feds indicted him for the banks, he hit during the crime spree. After he pled guilty, he received no jail credit, because he was considered to be in state-custody for those first, three years. His twelve-year sentence didn't start until the black robed, life changer banged the gavel.

My friend considered himself lucky he didn't get the max sentence he faced. So, he never pushed the jail-credit issue, but I believe his lawyer failed him. He had a good argument for those three years counting. Talk to your attorney, if you find yourself in a similar situation.

C. Showing Remorse at Sentencing

Some prison consulting firms make this their prime focus in the advice they give clients. I've watched YouTube videos where these guys make unrealistic promises that they can guarantee shorter sentences, if their clients demonstrate remorse to the judge before sentencing. Don't get me wrong. I also recommend entering the courtroom with this contrite attitude, but I won't go so far as to promise it will make the judge go easier on you.

First, judges, in most cases, are bound by mandatory minimum sentencing laws. I've read many court cases where the judge actually told the defendant that he wished he could grant a downward departure but was bound by strict laws to impose a harsher sentence than he wanted. Still, it wouldn't be a good idea to be disrespectful, curse, or act unrepentant at any time in the courtroom.

In less serious drug cases, and potentially with white-collar crimes, judges may have more discretion at sentencing. If you can demonstrate remorse with a well-crafted letter or video, and even have a character witness or two do the same, it could net a positive result in the court room. I can't say how much. I can't promise it will provide any, but it couldn't hurt. This will be your only chance to present a different version of yourself than the interpretation the prosecution has offered. My firm stands ready to help clients make the most of this opportunity.

D. Financial Obligations

1. Ask for a Delay till Your Release on Fines and Restitution

Your attorney should be able to predict the probability fines will be imposed against you at sentencing. If your crime defrauded victims, stole money outright, caused property damages, resulted in medical expenses, you definitely will face restitution penalties. If you know this is coming, have your lawyer prepped to ask for payment to be postponed until your release.

Your judge has complete discretion to grant this. If possible, come up with a narrative about your wife needing your limited resources for your children or something else appropriate. Explain how you will be able to focus on paying the debt when you get out and start working again. This might not work, but it's worth a shot, and sentencing the time to shoot it.

Under the *Financial Responsibility Program*, the FBOP can hound you for the money you owe throughout your bit. Though appellate courts have decided the Bureau can't force you to pay anything beyond a small assessment fee, around $50 per felony conviction, they found a way around these rulings. First, they create a payment plan and give you the choice of signing the contract or not.

Anyone who won't sign it is put on *FRP Refusal* status and faces several sanctions. You only will be allowed to spend $25.00 per month at the commissary. No matter your prison job, you will earn $5.25 per month. At some facilities, it might result in a cell move to a more crowded, less desirable space. If the prison has dorms, 12-men rooms, 6-men, 4-men, or 3-men, you'll never get to live in a two-person, or single-man cell. Basically, expect the worst accommodations available for as long as you refuse to cough-up any moolah. Since these things are considered privileges, not rights, they can use them to make your life uncomfortable.

The quickest fix is for a federal judge to exempt you from paying until your release. If you can make this happen, you may be able to avoid paying large fines altogether, because when probation ends, the feds spend little energy trying to collect money from ex-cons.

1. Renegotiate Child Support Arrangements

This next topic may be beyond the purview of your criminal attorney, or even the federal judge, but if you won't be able to meet your current child support or alimony payments, you need to consider approaching the appropriate court. Ask to have the payments canceled or decreased to a level you can swing while incarcerated.

E. Compassionate Release

Between the First Step Act and the CARES Act, compassionate releases have gotten easier to achieve than ever before. Although filing this on the day of sentencing would be too soon, you could ask your lawyer to bring up your eligibility then. Do it for no other reason than to plant the idea in your judge's mind, especially if you pled guilty, took responsibility, and showed remorse. Then you can file the paperwork at a more appropriate time after you reach your designated prison.

Some prison consulting firms offer to file this paperwork on your behalf. Be wary with this. Make sure anyone offering to file motions for you went to law school and are registered with the Bar Association. It's true that anyone can file a motion for you, even non-lawyers, but I wouldn't recommend using their help.

Here are the general requirements to be eligible for a Compassionate Release:

1. Qualifications

   a. Terminal Medical Condition: Incurable or Progressive Illness or Injury.
   b. Debilitated Medical Condition: Incurable or Progressive Illness or Injury
   c. Completely Disabled: Limited Self Care. In a bed or chair more than fifty percent of waking hours.

   a. Elderly:

   1. Seventy or Older. Been down thirty years or more.
   2. Sixty-five or Older. Chronic or serious medical conditions and has served fifty percent of sentence.
   3. Sixty-five or Older. Served the greater of ten years or seventy-five percent of term.

   a. Death or Incapacitation of Family Member Care Giver for Your Child

    Under Eighteen Years of Age.

   b. Incapacitation of Spouse or Registered Partner: Relationship had to be established before arrest.

The above requirements were lightened during the pandemic. Young men with questionable ailments received compassionate releases from 2020 forward. If you caught your case in a blue state, with a liberal judge, it might be worth it to try regardless of whether a new Covid (or other) strain is passing through the public or not, but don't bother if you have a sex charge or a crime of violence. Neither type prisoners are eligible. The Bureau will process a request made by another person on your behalf too. I recommend using an attorney.

Beyond the above requirements, you need a release plan. If you are sick, do you have insurance or money to pay for expenses? Can you work a job? Do you have a home? Family?

2. Compassionate Release Process

Your initial request goes to your prison's warden. If he or she decides to help, it gets sent to the General Counsel. If he or she endorses it, it goes to the FBOP's Director. I wouldn't expect success with this route though.

Of the 10,940 who applied in March through May of 2020, wardens approved 156. Higher-ups in Washington reviewed 84 of these and reversed all but 11. So, you can see how dismal prospects once looked. In fact, most wardens just throw the paperwork in the trash and never give the inmate an answer, not even a refusal. Without a formal denial, prisoners could not go forward with the appeal process.

Thankfully, changes have been made to the process. Now, you file with the warden and wait thirty days. No response from the warden within that time limit is considered a denial. At that point, compassionate release paperwork can be filed with your sentencing judge. I recommend sending an email notifying the warden via TRULINCs at the same time you submit the print copy. This creates an electronic paper trail verifying you took the correct steps.

The new law puts the power in your sentencing judge's hands. Since discretion has been limited by harsh mandatory minimum sentences, some liberal-minded judges have used compassionate releases as a way to rectify what they consider unjust punishments. In fact, new case law has encouraged judges to alter unfair sentences in this manner. If your judge made any comments about his hands being-tied, or about regretting having to give you so much time, at your sentencing, you may want to give a compassionate release motion a try. The worst thing that could happen is a denial. Talk to your attorney about the matter.

F. Prison Designation

1. Hardship Requests

The prison you get designated to is another subject you can ask your lawyer to bring up at sentencing. A recommendation from your judge that you be housed at a particular complex carries weight. I'll admit, it isn't binding on the Federal Bureau of Prisons, but it will increase your chances. The main obstacle will be if you have witnesses or victims already doing time at the facility you would like to reach. You can't go anywhere that holds inmates who filed separatees against you.

The First Step Act of 2018 directed the FBOP to place inmates within 500 driving miles of home. The problem with this directive is that many states do not have federal prisons. Others do not have every custody level. For instance, North Carolina has everything but a penitentiary. Tennessee doesn't have a low or pen.

Hardship requests can be made in two ways. First, you can ask the judge to make a recommendation for the prison closest to your home. The best incentive for this is to be near your children or an immediate family member with a documented illness or debilitating condition or handicap.

Second, if you have a serious medical condition or handicap, request a transfer to a Federal Medical Center. This guarantees better health care and usually a softer incarceration experience like better living conditions (potentially, even single man cells) and better food. See if any of these FMCs are close to you:

- Butner, NC
- Devens, MA
- Fort Worth, TX
- Lexington, KY
- Springfield, MO

2. Program Designation

You can also ask your sentencing judge to recommend programs which can get you designated at the closest prison to home carrying the curriculum. This is a really good idea if you are First Step eligible, because you will begin to earn a year off your sentence more quickly than transferring to a normal prison, waiting for orientation to get scheduled and then finally signing up for your initial program as long as six months after sentencing.

    a. BRAVE (Bureau Rehabilitation and Values Enhancement) Program
    - FCI Beckley, WV
    - FCI Victorville, CA

This is a six-month residential program offered to the newly convicted. To be eligible, you have to be under thirty-five, have more than a five-year sentence, and be your first time in prison. They want guys fresh out of county, as soon as they step off the weekly transfer bus.

The program's primary purpose is to help the newly convicted adjust to incarceration. It focuses on young guys, because these men typically are the most violent. It also targets those with long sentences, because they tend to have greater issues with negative emotions and frustration. The course seeks to channel that energy in a positive direction.

When I first came into the system, my custody points designated me to go to a US Penitentiary, but staff placed a management variable on me and assigned me to the BRAVE Program at FCI Beckley. Taking the program allowed me to start my sentence at a medium. If your custody points will be high due to the factors I discussed in the Pre-Sentence Investigation Section, this may be an option to dodge going to a pen.

Otherwise, taking BRAVE can get you shipped to West Virginia or California. In addition, BRAVE enrolls participants into the forty-hour drug program which will cover any court ordered rehab. Even better, they claim completion will win you a favorable transfer to a prison of your choice, though Beckley didn't offer me this perk.

b. RDAP (Residential Drug Abuse Program)

A judge's recommendation for RDAP will not guarantee you the year off, if you did not confess your drug or drinking problem during your Pre-Sentence Investigation or if you have a sex charge or crime of violence. The order won't fix that error, but a recommendation of this sort might net you a favorable designation at a prison of your choice. Some facilities don't offer RDAP. If your judge is willing to help, you may get into the program more quickly. This is important if you have a short sentence, thirty-six months or less. Otherwise, you'll face another transfer soon after getting comfortable at your first prison, and you may not have time to earn the entire reduction from that and the First Step Act.

A.   SOMP (Sex Offender Management Program)

If you have a sex case, you face a more difficult experience than most other federal prisoners. Some pedophiles come in so scared, they create elaborate ruses to stay safe. One child molester at FCI Petersburg faked paralysis.

When he first got arrested, he claimed he couldn't walk. He refused to do it when ordered by medical staff. He wheeled himself around in a chair for years, thinking his faked handicap would prevent guys from hurting him. It backfired in the sense that he gained sixty pounds and contracted Type II Diabetes through the inactivity.

If you fear harsh treatment because of your crime, tell your judge you would like to enroll in a treatment program as soon as possible. Sex offender programs are placed on protective custody yards. If you go to one of these facilities, as many as sixty percent of the prison population also will have sex cases. In addition, the other forty percent know they face new cases, not just in-house sanctions, for hurting pedophiles.

These are the safest places for child molesters to do time. Also, getting into a sex offender treatment program is the best way to avoid a civil commitment when your sentence expires. Take the program. Take it seriously. Fix whatever led to those compulsions. Rehabilitate and never repeat those actions.

Here are your options for facilities:

- USP Tucson, Az (High Custody)
- USP Marion, Il (Medium Custody)
- FCI Marianna, FL (Medium Custody)
- FCI Petersburg, VA (Medium Custody)
- FCI Elkton, Oh (Low Custody)
- FCI Englewood, Co (Low Custody)
- FCI Seagoville, Tx (Low Custody
- FMC Devens, Ma (Admin)
- FMC Carswell, Tx (Admin)

Compared to other facilities, sex offenders have a much easier incarceration experience at these spots.

Part Four: Day One: Self Surrendering or Arriving on the Weekly Transfer Bus

This book covers the most stressful period for federal prisoners: the conviction process on through the first, three months in custody. *Day One* at your designated facility will probably be the most intense for you. Fear has a lot to do with the unknown.

Will I get convicted? Will I go to prison? For how long? Will I be safe? Will my family be okay without me? Will they be waiting for me when I get out? Will she be screwing someone before the first week is out?

Fear diminishes a great deal once the facts become clear. That's true even when the facts suck. This section will shed light on your initial day as a federal prisoner. I can't make the experience more fun for you, but I can prepare you so it won't be a mystery you have to unravel on your own.

Beyond that, I'll provide advice for avoiding friction and staying safe. I'll give some tips to ease your transition. Most importantly, I'll explain how federal prison operates.

A. Initial Screening at Receiving and Discharge (R & D)

If you ride in on a bus, shackled along with fifty other cons designated to the same prison, you will go through most of the following your first day, definitely through your first week, but if you self-surrender, you will enter the prison by yourself. Because of this, there will be less staff on hand to process you, and it may take a few weeks to phase through the entire screening process.

Receiving and Discharge will be your first stop when entering a prison, whether as a new fish, a transfer from another yard, returning from a medical trip, or getting back from an appearance in court, resentencing, appeal hearings, or a state writ. This also will be your final stop before you *crown the chain-link womb* on your last day in prison too. Aside from your release, every time you enter R&D, the first thing that happens is a strip search.

I recommend a *wind mill* at this point. Once you're butterball, interlock your hands behind your head and wiggle your hips to spin the fan. Just kidding. Don't do that unless you want your ass kicked.

After bending over and coughing, they will provide a transfer outfit: T-shirt, khaki pants with an elastic band, boxers, and blue, canvas shoes. Inmates call them, *Jackie Chans*, and they make a great pair of slippers if you can sneak them back to the cellblock. If they don't send you to laundry on Day One, you should be able to keep them. Just see if someone in your car will loan you a pair of sneakers when you go to laundry the next morning.

Aside from the manual search, you also face an electronic one. The machine works like those the TSA has. You stand on it, and it puts a *Ken Doll*, naked image on the computer screen. If you are contemplating suitcasing a shank or some drugs, don't. if they see anything suspicious, they will go ass-mining immediately.

Beyond that, you will be photographed, fingerprinted, and if it isn't already on file, cotton swabbed for DNA. The photograph will be used to make an inmate identification card. You'll have to scan the ID to get a tray in the chow hall, pass through metal detectors on high-security yards, show it to receive your mail, and produce it whenever a staff member is looking for you.

B. Screenings by Department

Normally, someone from each of the following departments will set up in an office at R&D when a bus arrives. It won't happen if you self-surrender though. In that case, you might meet with one or two, and the rest will place you on *Call Out* over the next couple of weeks.

1. SIS (Special Investigative Services)

SIS is the rent-a-cop service that polices inmates *and* staff. They investigate alleged crimes by prisoners, as well as by federal employees at every facility. They can initiate in-house sanctions against cons who break the rules, but any serious charges get filed by the FBI.

An SIS employee will interview you before you are allowed to enter general population. In a private setting, they will ask you if you testified against anyone, evaluate any separatee you have filed or want to file, and question you about any fears you may have. It is their responsibility to enforce separatees, which keep you on separate compounds from any other prisoner who might want to hurt you.

If you are a sex offender, SIS will tell you whether you should have any concerns about safety at that prison. SIS will recommend protective custody in the hole, if they think you might be hurt. Just be honest and listen to them for the best results.

SIS also keeps rival gangs separated. Norteños will get jumped on a Surreño yard and vice versa. They will strip you and photograph suspicious tattoos, especially any that hint at gang affiliation.

While I'm on that, be careful of the tattoos you choose. You don't want to get a design a gang thinks represents them. For example, if a white racist shows up with a swastika, or thunderbolts, he might have trouble from the Aryan Brotherhood. These guys get pissed when inmates have *work* they didn't "earn". Likewise, some Mexican gangs will get upset if random inmates have Aztec symbolism inked onto their bodies. The groups would either jump the offender or hand him a shank and tell him to stab a rat or chomo. This act would then entitle him to wear the tattoo.

SIS goes through your prison record with you. They look at past bits and whatever happened while locked up on your current case. For instance, I was in an eighty-man brawl at FCI-Beckley. It got me shipped to USP Leavenworth. Before I was allowed into general population there, I had to assure SIS I wasn't afraid about retaliation from the friends of the guys I fought. He also warned me not to cause any trouble at his prison.

2. Medical Screenings

a. Bottom Bunk Passes

You will meet with a doctor before entering general population. If at all possible, use this opportunity to get yourself a bottom-bunk pass. This will matter a great deal at some prisons, but not so much at others. Generally, if you don't have a bottom-bunk pass, you will be assigned to the top bunk in a cell with an inmate who does have a pass, and maybe not always, but usually, these guys make the worst cellies.

Think big fat sloths who will fart up the small space day and night. If not that, you'll get stuck babysitting a sick or elderly inmate who never leaves the room, meaning no sanctuary for yourself, and no privacy ever. Many of these types are on psych meds and sleep seventeen-plus hours per day.

They tend to be less clean with their space and their bodies than other prisoners. Some have Darth Vader-sounding, sleep apnea, breathing machines and snore like congested bulldogs. Some get up ten times a night to flush the extremely loud toilets and piss on the floor in the process.

Maybe this sounds insensitive, but your prison experience will be three times as stressful, if you stuck with a bad cellie. Here are a few ways to get your own bottom bunk pass:

- Documented physical handicap
- Documented back trouble (Self-surrender with a note from your orthopedist.)
- Knees issues (Likewise, get a note)
- Documented sleep walking or prescribed medication with similar side effects

- Medication that makes you sleepy. Anything that could cause you to roll off the top bunk while passed out.
- Documented Vertigo
- Senior citizen
- Obese
- Documented Head Trauma

Get creative. Get verification from a doctor, and prison staff won't give you any trouble. Some guys get first floor passes too, bottom bunk with stairwell restrictions. They live in housing on first floor cells in ground level cellblocks.

I won't lie. It's possible, you might have a little friction on Day One, if a guy without a pass gets booted from his bottom bunk to accommodate you, but it's still worth it. If it happens, apologize to the man. Explain your ailment and promise him you'll move when other accommodations open up.

You probably won't need to follow up on that promise. He'll get used to the switch in a day or two. Just show respect to him and everyone else in your block.

b. Continuing Treatment from the Street

If you are self-surrendering, bring whatever medicine you are prescribed. You'll have a chance to talk to a doctor or PA pretty quick. Some scripts are banned no matter what. You won't get any opioids unless you face a terrible injury, surgery, or illness and most likely, will have to be housed at a Federal Medical Center.

Normal prisons won't give you anything stronger than Ibuprofen 800s. My cellie had major liver surgery. When he got back from the hospital, he received three Percocets the first day, Tylenol 3s for two days, and then Ibuprofen 800s.

You won't get Xanax, Valium, or Klonopin. They do offer psychotropic options, if you received this type of treatment on the street. You'll see a psychologist when you arrive to discuss these matters.

I have seen guys continue taking hormone replacement for low testosterone, but only if they were already on it. I also have seen transgenders continue estrogen treatment as well. You'll get an idea where you stand with staff on these issues during that initial screening.

This screening will approve or deny any medical aids you claim you need as well. The doctor will okay your prescriptions glasses. Every prison has a different stance on contacts. Normally, they are prohibited by the FBOP unless "ophthalmologic" clearance is indicated in the medical record. I would recommend bringing two pair of eyeglasses when you self-surrender. You don't want to end up wearing the Bureau safety goggles issued to indigent inmates.

During this screening, get approval for anything else you need: hearing aids, wheel chair, walker, cane, breathing machine (for sleep apnea), special footwear, braces, and anything else you'll need to survive in there. Also, if you have allergies or dietary restrictions, discuss that. Diabetics get a snack for late night sugar crashes. Some chronically ill inmates get cans of Ensure. The more paperwork from your doctor/s verifying your claims, the better.

The initial medical screening won't go much further than this. If you have health issues, you will be assigned to Chronic Care. This guarantees you will be called to medical for regular checkups without having to sign up for sick call first. Some prisons do initial dental screenings, but don't hold your breath for that.

c. Psychology Screening

More than anything, this screening determines your mental state as you enter prison. Claiming suicidal thoughts will get you placed in a padded room with a specially trained inmate observer who is supposed to watch you in case you make an attempt on your life. Psychology offers treatment and meds for behavioral and emotional problems. It also offers help for substance abuse problems, as well as sexual abuse problems

C. Bed Roll and Laundry Issue

1. Bed Roll

Some facilities will hand both of these out as soon as you arrive. Generally, if you self-surrender early in the day or your bus arrives before lunch, this will be the case. Otherwise, you'll get the bed roll when you arrive and go to laundry after breakfast the next morning for your issue there.

Typically, bed rolls have two sheets, one or two blankets, and maybe a pillow. Rules on pillows vary. Some prisons give you one. Some consider them contraband. In those, inmates pay someone to sew pillows from torn bedsheets and mattress stuffing. Then, they try to keep them hid during shakedowns. Some institutions issue sleep pads that have a pillow stuffed inside the mattress's lining.

The bed roll also includes an indigent bag. This is prison-issue hygiene items: crappy toothpaste, a three-inch toothbrush, soap, deodorant that doesn't work, and some places give flip-flops for the shower. If you don't have any money coming in from home, you can get one of these bags once or twice a month, but you're better off getting a job and buying stuff from commissary.

2. Laundry Issue

You'll get to visit laundry the first or second day. There will be khaki uniforms for inmates at mediums, lows, and pens, though some pens now use jumpsuits. Prisoners get green ones at camps. Most guys keep one pristine uniform for visits. Some find inmate tailors to make adjustments, like tapered, fitted jumpsuits, or high waters for the Muslims.

In the past, steel toe boots were issued and considered a mandatory part of the uniform. That has changed in many facilities, because prisoners use the heavy shoes as weapons when they knock opponents to the ground. Now many places only allow inmate workers to wear the safety boots. In their place, some institutions hand out thick-soled Velcro-fastened, orthopedic shoes. If you take a pair home with you, you'll fit right in at the nursing home. Thankfully, commissaries sell sneakers to wear in their place.

Your laundry issue alone does not provide sufficient clothes for comfort. Usually, you'll get two towels, two washcloths, three pairs of boxers, three T-shirts, and three pairs of calf length socks. If you want additional pairs of this stuff, inmate laundry workers will sell whatever you request in exchange for postage stamps.

You'll also need to buy stuff from commissary. That topic requires its own section. I'll help you get an idea about the initial expenses you'll need in a bit.

D. More First Day Concerns

1. How to Handle a Bad First Cellie

Hopefully, you'll b e able to pull off a bottom bunk pass. If not, most likely, you'll be assigned to a top bunk somewhere. Depending on the facility, you may have issues if your counselor assigns you to share a room with someone outside your race.

Prisoners segregate by choice and by established history. Racism exists throughout the federal system. No matter the color of your skin, you will feel its effects at some point. It usually gets worse as you go up in security.

Staff understand this. So in pens, they cell you with your own race. Other prisons vary. Some mediums do like pens. Others mix guys. The lows and camps pretty much lump everyone together. If you get assigned to a room with someone from a different race, introduce yourself. Ask your new cellie if he is okay with you bunking in his room. Some guys won't care. Some will. If he seems less than friendly, tell him you'll find other accommodations. Just ask him to bear with you a few days until you can find somewhere to move.

If you end up with an asshole, he might tell you to beat it. He might not even let you come in the cell to drop your things on your rack. Hopefully, it won't happen, but if it does, you basically have three options. First, you can pop him in the jaw. Obviously, this is a bad way to start out on a new compound. Aside from all the other reasons, if you just got there, he probably has more friends than you.

The last two options involve approaching a staff member about the situation. From a prison-etiquette perspective, there is a right way and a wrong way to do it. An *inmate* would approach a guard and say: "My new cellie said I can't live with him. If I go in there, he is going to hurt me."

If you do this, you will be labelled a *jailhouse snitch*. The guy might get sent to the hole, and you will have made an enemy of him, his friends, and every other prisoner that follows the convict code. It could even backfire and get you sent to the hole for protective custody. Which way it goes will depend on the lieutenant-on-duty during that shift and how he feels about rats.

A *convict* would approach a guard and say, "I'm not trying to create any problems, but I need a cell move. I can't bunk there. Sorry." He may take another prisoner with him to verify that is all he says. He may or may not add any information to that, but if he did, he would reveal nothing to put blame on the other inmate.

Unfortunately, this might bring consequences too, and I understand how unfair it sounds when I tell you to protect the bully from trouble, but this option is definitely preferred to the others. Worst case, you will get an incident report and get sent to the hole for refusing a direct order, but there is a good chance they will simply find you another cell. Even if you go to the SHU (Special Housing Unit), it will create less problems in the long run. Everyone will hear how you handled the difficult situation, and it will earn you respect. It might not turn the racist asshole into a friend, but it will prevent him becoming a hostile enemy.

Fortunately, situations like these don't happen every day. It's most likely going to happen to a child molester or known rat. Let's face it, moes have a look. If you're an older white guy who looks like he belongs in a barbershop quartet more than in a pair of handcuffs, you may get profiled.

Some men will not let a pedophile in their cells even for a couple minutes. On the bright side, most sex offenders start at lows, or Protective-Custody Mediums where things are more relaxed. So, if this label applies to you, you may still avoid problems.

In over two decades in prison, I never had things get that tense on day one on a new compound with a new cellie. I even got placed in two cells with black men who didn't want me living with them, but both gave me a few days to find somewhere to move.

It really depends on the guy. My first cellie at Yazoo City was a black Muslim. He had been down as long as me, and we got along fine. We lived together for six months, mostly locked down, 24/7, on Covid quarantines.

Just be polite. Communicate and don't give orders or ultimatums. Remember, you're the new guy on the block, but always refuse to wash another man's drawers, no matter how scary *and* horny he looks. Relax, I'm just kidding.

I'll address cellies soon. In that section, I'll give some advice about making things work smoothly while sharing an 8' by 11' cell, or smaller, with a guy you just met.

2. Cars

a. General Information

Cars are groups of men from the same state who stick together for protection. Cars matter less the lower you go in security level. In some lows and camps, the concept has died out.

If cars run the compound you land on, guys will ask you where you're from as soon as you arrive. Then, they'll point you to one of your homeboys. After that the homies you will meet will introduce you to the rest in your cellblock, and later to the guys on the yard.

Day One, you car will give you the grand tour. They will show you where to sit in the chow hall. They will find you a spot to place your chair in the common area or in their TV room. If there is a weight pile, and you have an interest, they will find you a time slot and workout car to join.

These will be the guys to answer your questions about the facility. Some of them will have been there for years. They will understand everything about how the place runs. They will dump you with information overload, even fill you in on the gossip about the guards' private lives and extra-marital affairs.

If you go to a camp, or a low without cars, someone will introduce himself and help you out with the above-mentioned stuff. Guys are bored in there. You always can count on someone wanting to show the new fish around.

Two other issues need to be discussed when considering cars, but they are important enough to have their own sections. So, I'll cover them next.

b. How Cars are Involved with Checking Paperwork

I covered checking paperwork earlier, but I wanted to add a few more comments here. If you ever face pressure about your sentence, charges, or level of cooperation, it usually will come from members in your car. On paperwork yards, your car won't accept you until they have verified you aren't a rat or sex offender. If you refuse to show anything, they will assume the worst.

Most of the time, they give you an option to check in, to request protective custody. This allows them to get rid of you without getting in trouble or beating you up. If you refuse to hand over your paperwork, and ignore their order to go to the hole, you may have a lopsided fight on your hands.

It won't just be lopsided. You won't see it coming. You'll be watching TV with headphones masking the sound of their approach. They might wait until you're lying in your bunk.

All this won't get decided or acted upon on your first day. So, relax. Unless someone on the compound knows you, or was with you in county jail, you won't get jumped in the first twenty-four hours. You *will* learn where you stand though. If someone wants to see your *work*, he will ask you soon after introducing himself.

At camps and most lows, if you offer to show your paperwork, most guys will say: "Don't worry about that. We don't do that here." If you hear that, you don't have to worry about anyone bothering you. They probably are terrified you are going to ask to see theirs.

If you are scared over your charges or level of cooperation, just wait. Even if someone demands to see your paperwork, they won't expect to see it right then. They know you don't have it on you.

Transfers don't have their property yet and new fish don't have anything when they self-surrender at the facility. You'll have time to figure out whether the guy who asked even matters too. Sometimes fake tough guys want to make a false impression, and they try to intimidate the new guys.

Bottom line, unless someone has overtly threatened you, give it a couple days to feel the environment out. If you check into protective custody, you will mark yourself for future yards. That type stuff follows you from prison to prison. You also set yourself up for a hard bid in the hole under twenty-three-hours-a-day lockdowns, and the hour of rec you get will be in a tiny fresh air cage in the SHU.

You'll learn from your SIS interview whether you landed on a dangerous yard or not. If you cooperated, you risk the most harm from those you testified against, and you won't have to worry about them until you get out. No matter what you do though, guys will figure out your past.

Convicts are nosy, and the system is small. The guys in your case will spread the word. The men you told on will pass your name and "sins" around every yard they hit. The cons you were locked up with in county will pass the word too. Plus, there are no secrets on the internet, and every cellblock has multiple smartphones and guys with subscriptions to *Pacer.*

These days, rats are prevalent at every yard. Conspiracy laws give you the option to become a rat or surrender your entire life. Rats might have a more difficult time, but they make it through their sentences just like everyone else. They stand a much greater chance of getting hurt after they get out of prison.

If you have good paperwork, there is no harm in showing it. I always offered mine to anyone who wanted to see it when I hit a new yard, but nobody saw mine without producing theirs. A lot of undercover rats in prison try to take the heat off themselves by exposing others. It's a common misdirection and a cue that someone might be a snitch.

c. Care Packages

I've read some prison survival books that warn inmates never to accept anything from another convict. It's true that some predators groom, or soften, targets into letting their guards down, by giving them stuff in the early stages. Inmates most at risk for this type treatment mostly include: homosexuals, transgenders, effeminate prisoners, and young, small-framed, timid, kids doing their first bids. Having said that, this grooming/gifting routine some predators use is different from initial care packages.

Most cars put care packages together for new arrivals. They only do this for homies. Typically, a care package will have basic hygiene items and a few snacks. Since many prisons don't give inmates flip-flops, and you can't take a shower without a pair, most care packages include them. There are not strings attached to these gifts, but they will expect you to replace the items for future homies once you get on your feet.

Aside from that, the FBOP is a small system. Even if you transfer to a camp or low where cars don't do this, chances are good that you'll run across someone from your previous prison or who you met in county. Guys look out for friends when they first arrive. This could include care packages. Cons also allow newbies to borrow spare sneakers and sweats until they can purchase their own or their property gets mailed to R&D from their previous facility.

Things will be different if you're just entering the system. If you're self-surrendering at your first institution, you probably won't know anyone when you get there. That's okay. There are generous men in every prison in America. Don't be afraid to accept an act of kindness.

Inmates will warn you about any predators or thieves in you cellblock, but having said that, be wary of anyone who tries to do constant favors for you or offers gifts frequently. Also, watch out for guys wanting to borrow something every day.

Some of these guys are just mooches. Maybe you have money and don't mind helping broke guys out, but be careful. Some predators condition inmates into saying yes through a long-series of small favors. They might have a secret agenda for locker theft, fraud on larger-scale, or sexual abuse.

If you become suspicious of anyone, ask other convicts about the person. Dirty secrets don't stay hidden on a compound for long. You'll be able to figure out pretty fast who to avoid. Most guys will warn you before you ask: "Watch out for that dude. He likes to flash his hose at anyone he can corner in the bathroom at rec."

Part Five: Week One in Custody

A. Unit Team

Unit team is a management concept used by the Federal Bureau of Prisons to place staff in direct proximity to inmates assigned to their unit. Each Unit Team includes a Unit Manager, Case Manager, Correctional Counselor, Secretary, and at least one Unit Officer. Psychologists and Educational Advisors are also available. The Unit Team staff offices usually are located in the cellblock so staff and inmates have access to each other.

B. Open House

A member of the Unit Team is supposed to be at the institution weekdays from 7:30 AM to 9:00 PM and during the day on weekend and holidays, but don't count on them ever meeting that requirement. Counselors and case managers are supposed to hold *Open House* every day they work. This is an hour period where inmates can approach them in their offices to ask questions.

If you end up with a staff member that actually does this once per week, count yourself lucky. Mr. Rodgers at USP Yazoo did it once or twice per month. A word of advice, don't go to them with frivolous complaints. Wait until something important comes up.

Unit Team members also are required to stand mainline occasionally. This is the lunch meal on weekdays. You can approach these employees in the chow hall during this period.

C. PATTERN Score

1. Generic

Each inmate will be classified initially by his Unit Team within twenty-eight days of his arrival. The First Step Act offers some inmates the opportunity to earn a year off their sentence. Eligibility is determined by charges and PATTERN (Prisoner Assessment Tool Targeting Estimated Risk and Needs) Score. If you have violence, a sex crime, or a non-violent gun charge, you are not eligible.

The Urban Institute created an app to help you determine PATTERN Score: Go to: apps.urban.org

2. Here is a look at the violent crimes that exclude an inmate from earning First Step Credit:

Violent Offense Codes for PATTERN Risk Assessment

* Category Federal Offenses such as (below) and/or any qualifying military or non-federal offenses

Aircraft and Motor Vehicle Offenses 18 USC 31 – 34, 36, & 37 Arson 18 USC 81

Assault 18 USC 111 - 119

Biological/Chemical Weapons 18 USC 175, 229, & 2283

Child Abuse 18 USC 2258

Child Sex Trafficking 18 USC 1591

Drugs, Death or Serious Bodily Injury 21 USC 841

Explosives 18 USC 831, 832, & 842 - 844

Firearms 18 USC 922 - 924, 929; & 26 USC 5851 - 5872

Genocide 18 USC 1091

Homicide 18 USC 1111 - 1114, & 1116 - 1121

Kidnapping 18 USC 1201 - 1204

Jury/Witness Tampering, Retaliation 18 USC 1501 – 1510, & 1513

Mutiny and Riot 18 USC 1792

National Defense 18 USC 2385; 22 USC 2778; 42 USC 2077, 2122, 2131, 2274 - 2275, & 2284

Protection of Certain Identities 50 USC 3121

Protection of Unborn Children 18 USC 1841

Racketeering 18 USC 1925, 1951, 1958, & 1959

Robbery/Theft Robbery 18 USC 2113 - 2115, 2118, 2119, & 2213 Searches & Seizures 18 USC 2231

Sex Offenses 8 USC 1328; 18 USC 1591, 2241 - 2248, 2251 – 2252, 2421 - 2429, 4320; & 10 USC 920

Solicitation to Commit Crime of Violence 18 USC 373

Slavery, Peonage 18 USC 1581 - 1590, 1592, & 1597

Terrorism 18 USC 229, 1992, 2331 – 2339, & 8124P

Threats 18 USC 871, 879, & 1751

Violence 18 USC 36, 37, 351, 521, 2261, 2262, 2280, 2281, 2291, 2340; & 49 USC 60123(b)

War Crimes 18 USC 2441

*Due to changes in the law, including statutory revisions and judicial decisions, this list may be periodically revised and updated. It is recommended that readers consult their attorney to obtain advice about any legal matter

3. Male and Female PATTERN Risk Scoring:

Either use the app to tabulate your PATTERN Score or contact my firm, and we'll do it for you.

4. Risk Categories Based on PATTERN Score:

General Violent

Risk Category Men / Women Men / Women

Minimum -23 to 8 -24 to 5 -11 to 6 -11 to 2

Low 9 to 30 6 to 31 7 to 24 3 to 19

Medium 31 to 43 32 to 49 25 to 30 20 to 25

High 44 to 113 50 to 102 31 to 71 26 to 33

5. Days Earned Per Month for Programming at Each Risk Category

Minimum: 15 Days Per 30 Days of Programming

Low: 15 Days Per 30 Days of Programming

Medium: 10 Days Per 30 Days of Programming

High: 5 Days Per 30 Days of Programming

D. Counselor

1. Initial Interview

During this period, your counselor may call you to his or her office and lay down the gospel. You'll get warned to stay out of trouble and keep your cell *inspection-ready*, Monday-Friday, from 7:30 AM-4:00 PM. That means having your bed made, cell clean, with nothing beyond a religious book out on lockers or desk. Dress code varies by prison, but all will expect you to wear your uniform to lunch (Mon-Fri), classes and all callouts.

2. PAC and TRULINCS Access

Your counselor will give you your Personal Access Code PAC#) and Personal Identification Number (PIN#). You need those for phone and computer access, though thumbprints have replaced PINs now for the most part. In addition, he or she will help you get your thumbprint taken for commissary shopping and to activate unit computers. Also, you will give a voice sample to access the inmate telephone system.

3. Financial Responsibility Program (FRP)

a.   FBOP Acting as a Collection Agency

I discussed this earlier in the section on sentencing. There, I explained the best way to delay payments until release was to get an order from your judge. If you weren't able to do that, your counselor will determine how much you pay each month towards fines and restitution.

Here's what the FBOP has to say about it:

"The Bureau works closely with the Administration Office of the Courts and the Department of Justice. The Bureau administers a systematic payment program for court-imposed fines, fees, and costs. All designated inmates are encouraged to develop a financial plan to meet their financial obligations. These obligations may include: special assessments imposed under 18 USC 3013, court ordered restitution, fines, and court ordered obligations (e.g., child support, alimony, and other judgements).

"Unit Team staff assist the inmate with financial planning, but the inmate is responsible for making all payments required, either from earnings within the institution, or from outside resources. The inmate must provide documentation of compliance and payment to the Unit Team. If an inmate refuses to meet his obligations, the inmate cannot work in UNICOR, and can only receive maintenance pay of $5.25 per month."

Aside from that, if you go on FRP Refusal Status, you will live in the worst accommodations available at the prison. Years back, the Fourth Circuit ruled that the FBOP is not a collection agency. They can't force you to pay, but living in a two-man cell is considered a privilege.

They will punish you if you refuse to contribute. Some facilities have dorms, six-men, four-men, and three-men rooms. If those options exist, an inmate on FRP Refusal will never make it to a two-man or single-man cell.

In addition, inmates who refuse to pay get placed on commissary restriction. Each facility handles this differently. Some cut spending limits to $25.00 per month. Others hold the $25.00 limit, but only allow hygiene products to be purchased. A few prisons have even more severely limited choices of items allowed to be purchased.

b. How Payments Get Tabulated

They will do this assessment within forty-five days of arriving. The minimum payment an inmate with a fine or restitution can get assigned is $25.00 per quarter. As of now, Unit Team will exclude $75.00 per month from assessment for phone calls, emails, and a few hygiene products.

Here's a look at the calculation:

- $75.00 per month excluded from wages and personal money
- Total funds are determined over six months
- Subtract previous (if any) FRP Payments over the period
- Subtract $450.00 ($75 x 6)
- The remaining figure is fair game

c. Options for Dealing with Fines

1. UNICOR

If you agree to pay and get a job with UNICOR (Prison Industries), staff will confiscate half of your wages each month. This contract allows you to keep the rest. You also get to keep everything that gets sent to your account from home. Since there is no upward limit on what they'll take otherwise, UNICOR is the preferred option for many men with large fines or restitution.

The only problem is that UNICOR has closed many factories in the FBOP. Many facilities no longer have prison industries on their compounds. For many convicts, UNICOR factories weigh heavily in the decision-making process before requesting a transfer to a new prison.

2. Contracts

I. Live Small

The minimum payment counselors will impose is $25.00 per quarter. Counselors know you need money to survive inside. The cool ones will allow you around $1,000 every six months before they hike your fine. Ask your counselor what his or her limit is.

II. Another Option

I'm certainly not advocating you do this, but some convicts send money to other inmates and pay them a small fee to go to commissary for them. Others do it, because inmates only can spend $360.00 at the store each month. For guys who refuse to eat in the chow hall, the limit doesn't stretch very far.

There are obvious risks with this. The man, especially if he smokes deuce, may take your money and check in. You also may make yourself a target for locker theft or extortion by flashing a lot of money in the cell block.

The most likely result will be to get an incident report (a shot) for sending money to another prisoner, and if that happens, both of you will lose commissary privileges for around six months, as well as accrued good time.

E. Program Review

After initial classification, Program Review meetings will be scheduled by the Unit Team every 180 Days (Every 90 days your final year). At the initial classification, program goals will be established, education enrollment, participation, and progress will be examined, release plans will be discussed and the other pertinent information concerning your sentence, work assignment, and security level will be reviewed.

They always make a big deal about Program Review, but it only really matters in three ways: First, every eighteen months they are supposed to adjust custody points. This will matter if you are trying to do down in security-level: pen to medium, medium to low, or low to camp. The best ways to accomplish this is to: program, grow older, stay out of trouble, and take care of any outstanding detainers against you.

Second, if you are First Step Eligible, you should use this time to verify your time credits for the classes you've taken. Third, when you get short, eighteen months till release, Unit Team will submit you for halfway house placement and/or home confinement. Every program review you endure without these three options in play will be a complete waste of time, but unfortunately, attendance is mandatory. If you don't have any of the above options available, only speak when spoken to, sign the paper, and leave as fast as possible.

F. Getting Visitors Approved

1. PSR

Counselors handle this as well. They should review your Pre-Sentence Report (PSR) and automatically approve your immediate family listed in the document: spouse, children, parents, and siblings. They should but some don't. Others are just assholes who will demand a visitation form from everyone simply to hassle you.

2. Procedure.

Potential visitors can print visitor forms online, fill them out, and mail them. Otherwise, get a form from your counselor and send it to your friend or family member. Just make sure they mail it back to your counselor, NOT TO YOU. The address will be on the form.

The existence of a criminal conviction does not preclude visits. According to the FBOP:

"Staff shall give consideration to the nature, extent, and recentness of convictions as weighing against the security considerations of the institution..." Blah, blah, blah...... Unless the felon is an immediate family member, tell 'em you'll see 'em when you get out.

3. Common Occurrence When Submitting Forms

The form asks whether the person knew you before your arrest. Anyone who checks the *NO* box will be denied. I know guys who met future wives while incarcerated, but women marked *NO* on the form before mailing it.

My buddy spent eight years sustaining a relationship like this through emails, letters, and phone calls alone. He never got a face-to-face visit with his fiancé while locked up. Their first kiss happened the day of his release.

Officially, there is a policy. An inmate may request in writing to Unit Team for consideration for an exemption to the prior relationship rule. The warden makes the final decision. An inmate also may also ask the US President for a pardon. You have a roughly equal chance with both.

G. How Visitation Works

1. Basic Procedures

Once you've gotten your visitors approved, you need to understand how the process works. If you're coming from a county jail that only allowed you to talk on a phone for thirty minutes, while looking at your loved ones through plexiglass, you'll feel extra motivation for a contact visit.

No matter what the movies say, conjugal visits don't exist in federal prison. *Cellie lovin'* excluded, you can forget about sex, except in your dreams. You can hug and kiss your spouse at the beginning of a visit and again at the end, but some prisons won't let couples hold hands or even sit next to each other. Also, under Covid protocols, you can't touch, at all, no kisses, nothing. Under Code Red, they cancel visits altogether.

2. Visiting Hours

This varies between facilities, but you can count on every visitation room being open during the day on weekends and holidays (usually from 8:00AM-3:00PM). Some places also have night visits during the week between 5:00PM and 9:00PM. Days vary. Often, they'll choose between Monday, Thursday, and Friday nights, sometimes all three.

3. Point System

The point system restricts the number of visits allowed each month. It's main purpose is to keep locals living near the prison from filling every seat and guarantee space for inmates' families who have travelled a longways to come to the prison. The point system applies to every facility in the FBOP. (Many have modified this due to Covid, but hopefully, if your facility hasn't yet reinstituted the point system, it will soon; because the pandemic era was much more restrictive.)

Each inmate receives ten points per month. Points are charged as follows:

- Weekday visits = one point each
- Weekend visits = two points each
- Holiday visits = two points each
- No more than six points can be used on weekends
- Unused points are canceled at the end of each month
- Any part of a day counts as a whole day/point/s

4. Number of Visitors Allowed

You can have twenty individuals on your visitation list. Only ten can be friends. The rest have to be family. One inmate can have four visitors at one time. Children under two years of age, who do not require a seat, will not be counted against the total of four. Special permission can be requested for six visitors at once. This will be approved, if they travel a longways to see you, or if a family member has a documented, life-threatening illness.

Requests for special visits (extra people) should be directed to you unit manager. Most prison-orientation handbooks mention the availability of special visits based on family emergencies, but I can't remember this ever happening. I have seen special phone calls granted for deaths or to hospital rooms offered by chaplain staff though. I also have seen inmates get to watch videos in the chapel filmed at family members' funerals.

5. Dress Code for Visitors

The front entrance officer decides whether visitors are wearing suitable attire. They can be real assholes. I could add a hundred pages of stories about it, but one stands out in my mind.

My cellie's girlfriend, Kate, from New Zealand, flew to Virginia to see him. She took a cab to the prison and asked the driver to come back in five hours. The lady working visit that day refused to let Kate enter, because supposedly, her skirt was too short.

Kate went back outside carrying her two-year-old daughter on her hip. She had no car, and because they don't allow them inside the prison, no smart phone with her. She had to borrow one from a woman in the parking lot.

She called her cabbie back to the prison. She had to go to the mall, and then back to her hotel room, before returning to the facility. This shaved over an hour from her visiting time, aside from all the senseless expense.

During the second attempt, she passed the visual inspection, but the wire in her bra set off the metal detector. They wouldn't let her remove the undergarment and enter the visiting room. They wouldn't let her go in with it on either. She had to repeat the process with the cab and go on another shopping excursion.

She wasted a few hundred bucks in the process. My cellie stressed for the couple hours his girls were missing without knowing why. They only got to see each other for an hour before visitation closed for the day. It wasn't a good hour either with his woman irritated by the treatment and the baby fussy and needing a nap.

6. General Dress Code Guidelines:

- Shorts and Culottes are acceptable but no more than 3" above the knee.
- No see-through clothing
- No military- style clothing (e.g., camouflage)
- No tank tops or other wear that exposes the midriff or cleavage area
- Footwear is required. Sandals are acceptable with the exception of flip-flops.
- Skirts must be within 3 inches of the knee. No splits up
- No medical scrubs
- No spandex-type clothing other tightfitting apparel.
- No solid gray sweatpants or sweatshirts (nothing that matches inmate rec clothes)
- No solid khaki/tan clothing at the high, medium, and low facilities. (Nothing that resembles inmate uniforms)
- No solid green clothing for camp visitors

This list isn't all-inclusive. Check the specific rules at your prison before your family plans a visit.

Photo identification is required for visitors. These may include a valid driver's license, passports, military IDs, INS card, or state identification card. Birth certificates are not considered proper identification. Persons without proper ID will not be permitted into visitation.

Don't expect any leniency here. My aunt came to see me in West Virginia, from Carolina, with my mom and dad. She forgot her license and was forced to wait at the hotel all weekend.

7. Scanning

Visitors must be able to clear an x-ray. (Don't wear bras with metal in them!) Visitors with medical conditions which prevent them from passing through the metal detector or other conditions (e.g., oxygen tank, prosthetics) must have written documentation or prior approval through the inmate's Unit Team. Visitors' purses, attorneys' briefcases, etc., may also be searched. Other personal articles belonging to the visitors must be placed in lockers provided by the institutional or may be left in their cars.

Some prisons also employ drugs sniffers or ion scanners. If a visitor sets them off, he or she will be refused admittance. So, wait to break up those kilos until you get home. It may have a negative effect on the inmate too, like being placed in a dry cell or under SIS investigation. Even if the visitor is coming from a weed-legal state, marijuana still prohibited under federal law.

My buddy's mom was prescribed Xanax. She broke a pill in half in her car and took it to combat the anxiety entering the prison always caused her. The drug residue set off the scanner. She didn't bring a doctor's note for the prescription drug and was refused entry.

Visitors can't be forced to submit to the scanner; however, any who refuse will not be allowed in that day. Also, the next time they return, they will be scanned, as well as any visitors that come with that person.

Anyone who refuses, or sets off the scanner, faces these sanctions:

- First occurrence - visitors will be banned for 48 hours
- Second occurrence - visitors will be banned 30 days
- Third occurrence – banned for 90 days
- Fourth occurrence - banned for 120 days

A visitor who sets off the scanner will be scanned every time they return for one year, as well as anyone who comes with them. Visitors may appeal these decisions by following the procedures on the Notification of Denial Form (BP-S732). Inmates can use the administrative remedy process. (Without a doctor's note, either attempt will not get very far.)

8. Authorized items

a. From Visitors

Visitors are permitted to bring cash not exceeding $40.00 (Inflation may raise that soon!) into the visiting room to purchase items from the vending machines. Put the change in a clear bag or plastic container. Also, a reasonable number of diapers and other infant care items and sanitary napkins may be brought into the visiting room, and no food bought from the vending machines can be taken from the visiting room. Cakes with files baked inside will be confiscated on site.

Inmates are not allowed to receive either coins or money while in the visiting room. Money for commissary accounts must be sent to the national lockbox (or through Western Union). Visitors are not permitted to give the inmates any items other than food purchased from the visiting-room, vending machines. These items must be consumed in the visiting room and cannot be taken out of the visiting room by the inmate. (Pandemic protocol closed the vending machines and turned off the water fountains. If a new strain causes your facility to return to this state, visits will be short enough for hunger not to be an issue, probably one hour.) Even more likely, visits will be canceled altogether.

b. For Inmates

Inmates may only take a wedding band, photo tickets (if you want to take a picture with your visitors, you buy the coupons at commissary. They cost $1.00 per photo), prescription eyeglasses, and a religious medallion into the visiting room. Items brought in or purchased by the visitor may not be brought back inside the institution by the inmate. No items may be exchanged in the visiting room between an inmate and visitor.

If an inmate is suspected of receiving contraband, his visit will be terminated, and he will be strip-searched. Then, he will be taken to a dry cell. He stays there until he has had three bowel movements in a bucket. Each offering gets searched thoroughly.

Some institutions allow sneakers to be worn at visits. Some require inmates to put on facility-issued safety boots or orthopedic shoes with Velcro straps. Your orientation handbook will explain the prisons rules on this.

9. Special Rules for Children

As stated above, children two years and older, who require a seat, will be counted as an adult, as it relates to the number of visitors allowed in the visiting room. Children only, are permitted in the children's play area. Of course, most spots don't have play areas, or they tend to stay locked.

Some guards cause more problems than others when it comes to kids. It depends on the officer. Some relax and allow kids to run wild and screaming through the area. Some will issue warnings about simple stuff, like a child wandering over to other inmate groups or sitting on the floor. I have watched many visits get terminated over unruly toddlers.

Some guards will talk very disrespectfully to your family. Prepare your people in advance. At FCI-Beckley, a CO made rude comments about a prisoner's children and girlfriend before he kicked them out. In retaliation, the convict hospitalized the other officer while they were locked together in the strip-search room.

*KEEP AN EYE ON YOUR KIDS! *

Especially, at the lows. There will be child molesters in the visiting room. For a couple years at FCI-Beckley, inmates weren't allowed to hold children in their laps, because a pedophile had hurt a child in a prison in California. Don't let your children out of your sight!

10. Special considerations

a. Change out

You will always be strip-searched when you leave visitation. That's policy everywhere. I managed to avoid it maybe twice in twenty-plus years and only because the guard was lazy and knew I wasn't a rat. You will be patted down before your visit and strip searched when you return to your cellblock. When you're bent over with your cheeks pulled apart, I recommend you start singing, like Ace Ventura.

b. SHU (Special Housing Unit) Visits

Hole visitation protocol follows different procedures at every facility. Some refuse contact visits while in the SHU. All refuse visits for inmates serving time for breaking prison rules. Other people back there, in protective custody or waiting for a disciplinary hearing, may be allowed to see their families in person, or they may have to use the facility's closed-circuit TV system (or Skype). In that case, visitors use a screen in visitation. Inmates use one in the hole.

c. Covid

During the pandemic, visits were simply terminated. After the vaccine, family and friends were allowed in again under strict parameters: no contact, masks at all times, and social distancing from family. Visitors also had to submit to temperature checks when they entered. Only two visitors were allowed in the facility. Photographs weren't taken during this time either. Water fountains were disabled and vending machines were inaccessible. Honestly, you were better off making a phone call and letting them save the money for hotel, food, and gas.

d. Attorney Visits

These usually happen during weekdays when normal visitation isn't taking place. Arrangements are made in advance by the inmate's Unit Team.

H. Everything You Need to Know About Commissary

1. Fish Draw

Aside from seeing loved ones at visitation, getting a chance to shop is a top concern on every new fish's mind during *Week One*. Usually, inmates have an assigned weekday to shop. Sometimes, they rotate: weekly, monthly, or quarterly. Sometimes, they stay the same. Every prison does it a little differently.

A *fish draw* is a special privilege given to new arrivals. It allows them to go to commissary on the first available shopping day after they arrive. Ask an inmate in your cellblock if your prison allows first-time shoppers this privilege.

2. How to Receive Money

Inmates don't have access to cash. Deposits have to be made to the prisoner's trust-fund account. Inmates may check the balance of their account either by dialing 118+ PAC# on the inmate telephones in the housing unit or on a computer in the same area.

Funds must be sent to an authorized outside source through one of the following two methods:

a. National Lockbox

Federal Bureau of Prisons

Inmate's name

Inmate's Register Number

Des Moines, Iowa 50947 – 0001

Use this address for every prison in the system. Use a postal money. Regular money orders take an additional fifteen days to clear.

b. Western Union

- Use the Quick Collect Program
- westernunion.com
- Select: *Bill Payment*
- Then: *Quick Collect*

- Select: *Option 2*
- *"Pay to"* field should read: Bureau of Prisons
- *City Code: FBOP*
- *State Code: DC*
- Sender's account name should contain inmate's register number and committed name
- Or by credit card: 1-800-634-3422

3. Spending Limits

The Federal Bureau of Prisons established spending limits at commissary for several reasons. First, they don't want inmates to acquire excess property which could be used as currency for gambling, drugs, other contraband, or grant control over other inmates; nor, do they want small cells crammed with junk food. The administration hates clutter and anything that might create a fire hazard.

They also don't want convicts to hoard merchandise to open stores in their cells. That never works. Every cellblock in the system has at least three store men. These cons offer commissary items on-the-front or for stamps. Markups range between 25% to 100% of retail.

Some guards will take excess commissary or any property you can't produce a receipt for (TRULINCs keeps a record of every purchase you've ever made, but that doesn't help if someone else bought the stuff.) This will also happen on large-scale shakedowns, or any time SIS gets tipped off against you. If Special Investigative Services hits a store cell, they will take anything over the monthly limit, as well as excess stamps.

USP Yazoo City only opened commissary twice a month for gen pop. Petersburg Low allowed $90.00 in sales each week ($25 during the pandemic). FCI-Beckley would ring up the entire $360 in one go. Yazoo did $180 each shopping day. You just have to see how your spot does it when you get there.

Hole commissary rules very too. Yazoo shopped the hole every week, more than the compound. Some SHUs tell you you're hit till you leave the hole. Others let you shop a modified list as long as *no shopping* isn't a part of your imposed sanctions.

The good news on limits is that over-the-counter medication, vitamins (depending on facility), and postage stamps don't count against your limit. There is, however, a limit on stamps. Because they are currency (inmate legal tender) on every compound, staff do not want inmates hoarding them. Typically, you can purchase one to two flat books per week, more with a counselor's signature on a *copout* (Inmate Request to Staff, BP-148) for mailing legal work to courts, or books, hobby craft, and other personal property home. They usually will confiscate anything over three books (sixty stamps) they find on a person or in a cell.

Spending limits create an issue for new arrivals coming into the system fresh, with no property. The allotted limit won't buy everything you need to get comfortable. For this reason, some guys risk sending money to another inmate's account.

Guys usually find deuce-heads, junkies, and broke convicts with no funds or money coming from home. They provide the service for small fee, but you're taking a risk by doing this. First, junkies are notorious for getting the money put on their accounts and then checking into protective custody, or they just spend it all and then dare you to do something about it. Also, if you get caught by staff, which is likely, both of you will get incident reports, resulting in lost good time and commissary restriction (only $25.00 worth of hygiene and medicine for six months.)

Some guys don't care. They often get caught by talking about sending money to another prisoner's account on the inmate phone system. Every call is recorded. Plus, a guard is assigned to listen to calls as they happen live.

Usually, spending limits increase by $100 the final six weeks of each year. Most prisons create a holiday list with extra junk food to purchase. The limit hike is your Christmas present along with a small bag of snacks, and a few added items for sale on your commissary list.

Most prisons also change a few items on the commissary list (e.g., sodas, ice cream flavors, chips, and candy bars) every quarter. The lazier spots don't do it. Expect 80% of the food to be of the unhealthy gas station variety. Having said that, *a* future publication will cover how to make the most out of these limited items: *Calaboose Cooking: 200 Recipes to Make your Stay in Club Fed Better.*

4. What You Need to Get Comfortable

The initial purchases you need to make will burn through your spending limit pretty quickly. Some guys spread those items out over a couple months, buying the most important first. Others buy used stuff like: sneakers, sweats, shorts, watches, workout gloves, and braces from other inmates with stamps, commissary, or by sending money to their accounts.

Here's a look at what you need to get by:

- MP3 Player $88.40
- Tablet $110 or more
- Radio $38.55 (Cellblock TVs don't have speakers. You have to use a Walkman-style radio or MP3 player, but most guys prefer radios for television viewing to make MP3 players last longer.)
- Headphones $31.45
- Sweat Pants $19.50
- Sweat Shirt $23.40
- Shorts $13.30
- T-shirts $6.50
- Long-sleeved T-shirts $10.40
- Thermal Top $10.15
- Boxers $8.45
- Sneakers Averaging around $75.00
- Watch Timex $22.50
- Watch G- Shock $89.70
- Pad Lock $7.55
- Reading Lights $10.00
- Hygiene Items Around $70.00 to start
- Stationary Items Around $20.00 to start
- Bowls, Water Bottle, Coffee Cup, and Plastic Tableware Arounds $20.00
- Tile, Shower Cavity, Soap Dishes, and Shower Shoes Around $30.00

Your spending limit will be gone pretty quickly, and without buying extra food, expect to hear your stomach growling you to sleep each night. Also, if you land on a yard without air conditioning, or old, ineffectual ACs, you will need to buy fans, abouts $35.00 apiece. I had nine in my cell at Petersburg, and the room still average 94° every night through July and August.

5. Banned Items

When I came into the system in 2001, commissaries were closer to grocery stores and gas stations. They sold vegetables, bread, bananas, whole garlic, fruit juice, sugar cubes, beard trimmers, and lots of other items banned today ... like the prostitutes they used to bus in once a month, kidding. Most stuff gets axed, because it could be made into hooch or shine too easily.

These days sugar products get reduced by the month at commissary in the chow hall. Many places in the system sale diet soda, diabetic candy, and ban anything sweet enough to ferment easily. The strictest spots have replaced honey with a clear, artificial substitute, take my word for it when I tell you to never sample the sugar-free jelly. It will take a day to get rid of the aftertaste.

All tobacco products were banned in 2006. They outlawed matches a couple years beforehand. Now, some prisons have stopped selling batteries, because guys use them to light contraband smokes and hits of K2.

When the battery rule when into effect, residents at those facilities had to purchase new, wind-up radios, alarm clocks, and reading lights. It had zero effect on the junkies getting high. No one got reimbursed for the battery-powered appliances they had to throw in the garbage either.

6. Special Purchase Orders (SPOs)

These items affect spending limits like any other purchase. Big orders can throw off your entire month.

    a. Religious

After receiving chapel approval, inmates are allowed to order some personal religious property through commissary. Items include: rosaries, malas, prayer rugs, headwear, prayer oil, food during holy times (Jewish and Muslim), medallions, and anything else you can prove both essential to worship, and not a threat to the institution. The chapel will provide preapproved vendors available to take orders. Commissary will gouge you with a 30% markup over what the company charges, though.

    a. Hobby Craft

Recreation doesn't provide materials for individual pursuits. You have to buy them yourself. Most facilities allow inmates to shop from the Dick Blick catalog. You can order art supplies, material for ceramics, leathercraft, harmonicas, crochet, cross-stitch, and follow a bunch of other strange pursuits, like Popsicle-stick art. Commissary will hit you with 30% markup over retail on this stuff too. Approval for these items start with the rec officer assigned to SPOs for the quarter.

7. Commissary Fund Withdrawals (Sending Money from your Account)

Request for Withdrawal of Inmate Personal Funds, BP-199 forms, are processed by the Trust Fund Department (commissary, TRULINCS, and Laundry). Withdrawals are initiated in the TRULINCS Computer System. Choose: *Send Funds* (BP-199)

Once you fill it out and submit, you'll have to walk to the education building (or wherever the station is) and print a hard copy. Sign the paper in front of your counselor when you turn it in. He or she won't accept it if you already signed it. Unit Managers approve the withdrawal request. Only an Assistant Warden can okay withdrawals exceeding $500 or donations to charities.

On the computer, there will be a box marked: *Care of Cashier*. If you are ordering books, a newspaper subscription, or magazine scripts, click on the box. This will force the cashier to send a check to your counselor. Then, the check will be placed in an envelope you provide along with your order form for the desired product.

Leave the box blank if you are sending money to friends or family. A blank box will cause a check to be cut and mailed straight to your specified address. It happens much quicker than the previous way and send you a stamp.

8. Account Inquiries

As I said before, you can check your account balance on the computers in your unit, or you can dial "118+ your PAC#" on an inmate phone.

Also, make sure you check your receipt before you leave the store. The cops there are glorified cashiers, make frequent mistakes, and entirely too much money. I can't tell you how many times they ring up a single item more than once, like a bag of coffee fifteen times. It seems to happen to at least one inmate per shopping day. Get it fixed before leaving the commissary building, or they may refuse to do it.

More serious issues can be corrected by filling out a BP-148 (*Inmate Request to Staff*) to financial management at open house, through the inmate mail system, or send an email on TRULINCS.

9. Security

You have to supply thumbprint verification every time you shop. The scanner sits in front of the checkout window. This verifies who you are, and guarantees no one can rob you.

Some guys have trouble getting their prints accepted. It usually happens to old men and cons with extremely dry skin. If your thumbprint won't show up, they can use a different digit. Worst case, they can make you fingerprint exempt, and force you to show your ID card every time you shop.

I. Inmate Phone System

a. Basics

Inmates must add their contacts (Name, relationship, phone #, email address, and mailing address) to TRULINCS. You can put up to 100 contacts in TRULINCs, but only thirty total phone numbers are allowed. The FBOP wants information on everyone you plan to call, many guys input fake information. Phone calls last fifteen minutes at the longest. You have to wait between thirty minutes and one hour, depending on the facility, to use it again.

Phone Access Codes (PAC#S) should not be shared. Keep them confidential. The prison will charge you five dollars for each new one they have to give. For each phone call, you have to dial your PAC#, and pass computer voice verification, before the number rings. Usually, they prerecord your name and a prepared phrase like: *The United States of America*. Interestingly, saying, *Fuck the United States of America*, will still grant you access to the system.

b. Money and Minutes

Phone credits are transferred from your commissary account to your telephone account by dialing "118+ PAC #" and following the directions on the phone. You can check information by pressing:

- Commissary Balance: *#1*
- Phone Balance: *#2*
- Transfer Funds: *#3*

Inmates are restricted to 300 minutes calling each month. This is combined for collect and debit calling. The 300 minutes are reset based on the fifth digit in your registration number.

Formula for Revalidation:

(Fifth Digit X 3 +1) = Revalidation Date
(e.g., *3* X 3 +1) = Tenth of the Month

- Pre-Covid, locals cost $.90 for 15 minutes.
- Long Distance Cost $3.15 for 15 minutes.

Many men burn through their minutes talking to their girlfriends or wives the first week, and then feel miserable not hearing their women's voices for the rest of the month. Guys who can't make do with 300 minutes, buy extra ones from broke or addicted inmates who don't use the phone. Anyone caught doing it loses good time and phone privileges for six months. Most get caught within a month or two starting.

Inmates use Google Voice to acquire local numbers for frequently called friends and family members. For it to work, the number needs a matching area code and first, three digits to that of the facility. It won't work if they don't disactivate voicemail features, though.

Other inmates use companies, like *Phone Donkey*, to acquire local numbers. They also provide texting services, but the FBOP does not like these. They will suspend accounts and write incident reports if they catch you using a texting service.

c. Covid Rule Changes

During the pandemic, changes went into effect. First, because visits were canceled until the vaccine's creation, monthly limits were increased from 300 to 500 minutes. Second, they made all calls free. Even when they reinstated visitation, they continue the practice. In fact, it still is in effect, but for how long is anybody's guess.

d. A Word of Warning

Don't make threats on the phone. Don't try to conduct business. It is illegal for an inmate to run a business from prison, *any business*, even those not breaking other laws. I've seen old-timers who haven't been able to use the phone for decades for making threats or putting out hits over the phone.

You can catch a new case by threatening your spouse. They take it seriously. I remember listening to a guy in my cellblock scream at his old lady every day on the phone. He killed her and her young daughter within a week of release. Past experiences like this have made the administration more vigilant.

A crazy guy in my unit caught a new case with a similar situation. He mailed Obama a threatening letter to 1600 Pennsylvania Ave. He doused it with baby powder before sealing it. A federal judge attached ten years to the end of the sentence he was already serving, even though the guy needed psychiatric treatment, not more time. He died of liver failure before he finished the second sentence.

e. Blocked Numbers

Every time you make a phone call, the system will tell the people answering about the big, bad criminal in federal prison who wants to chat. Then, it offers three choices:

- To accept the call: Dial 5

- To refuse the call: Hang Up
- To block all future calls: Dial 7

Contacts who either intentionally or accidentally block phone or email accounts must submit a written notice to the Trust Fund Supervisor to unblock the phone/email utilizing the staff messaging function in TRULINCS. This notice must include a copy of the contact phone #and/or email address along with the inmates name and register #. Most likely, the supervisor will contact your friend and see how he or she feels about receiving calls or emails.

2. TRULINCS Computer System

a. Basics

Inmates access the TRULINCS system by typing their register numbers without the hyphen (on your ID card), Phone Access Code (PAC #, nine-digit code from your counselor), and scanning their thumbprint, or (Personal Identification Number (PIN#) a four-digit code from your counselor for guys who are fingerprint exempt). Here's what you can do on TRULINCS:

Purchase TRU-Units ($.05 apiece) for:

- Printing copies of legal materials or saved emails
- One TRU-Unit buys you one minute to read or type emails.
- Purchasing music: songs cost: 16, 24, or 31 TRU-Units (Mostly 31) each

- Public Messaging (Email)
- View Account Transactions (Free)
- Send Funds
- Sample and Buy Music – 30 Samples Per Day
- Contact List Management (100 Total Allowed) and him
- Portal Mailing List for labels (This was suspended during Covid, but in the past, you had to affix a mailing label to every label.) (Free)
- Electronic Law Library (Lexus\Nexus) (Free)
- Inmate to Staff Messaging (Free)
- View Local Documents (free)
- Skype

b. Locked Accounts

Some guys with chronically dry skin have trouble getting the thumbprint scanner to work, especially during winter months. The computer system will lock you out after so many failed attempts, usually no more than ten per machine. If you get blocked, it will last at least twenty-four hours or longer.

If this is a frequent problem, approached the ITS manager at open house and explain the situation. (If commissary has a cool CO, he or she can do it.) They will allow you to submit a different finger to scan. If that doesn't work, they can make you fingerprint exempt. In the latter scenario, you can access the computers with Reg#, PAC#, and PIN#.

J. Mail

a. General Rules

In most cases, inmates are permitted to correspond with the public, family members, and others without prior approval; however, all contacts have to be typed into your TRULINCs account. (This was suspended during the pandemic, but at some point, they will return to this.) From there, you have to print mailing labels with each contact's address.

Outgoing mail at low institutions and camps may be sealed. Inmates housed at mediums, penitentiaries, or in Special Housing Units (SHU) may not seal their outgoing correspondence. This latter mail is sealed by the unit officer when the mail is collected. Some will read your letters. Some inmates have their letters sent to Special Investigative Services (SIS) for special review.

The outgoing envelope must have the inmate's full committed name, registration number, and the return address on the upper left corner. The name of your institution must be spelled out entirely, no abbreviations. The FBOP wants to guarantee all recipients of your mail know where you are to cut down on potential scams and such.

No prison runs mail services on the weekend. Each passes out mail once per week day, usually after the 4:00 PM standing counts. They will do a verbal mail call or put out a list.

Inmates assume responsibility for the content of all their letters. Correspondences containing threats, extortion, etc., may be prosecuted. I've also seen inmates catch fresh federal sentences for tax fraud (sending in tax returns while incarcerated), scams/extortion (most often, finding vulnerable targets on homosexual, pen-pal services), and making threats to judges, prosecutors, defense attorneys, ex-wife, codefendants, and elected officials.

b. *WARNING* To Sex Offenders, those who have testified against others, or created enemies in other ways

*Do not accept any books at mail call that your family didn't order! Some dealers smuggle drugs inside hardback covers or are sprayed onto book pages. When they send it inside the prison, they ship it to unsuspecting pedophiles, rats, and/or anyone they don't like. When the package arrives, if staff doesn't catch it, they will force the recipient to hand it over. If the mailroom catches it, the recipient will get in trouble over it, and he won't know who really ordered it.

c. Banned Items from Incoming Mail

Inmates are not allowed to receive stationary items (letterhead materials, writing pads/paper, blank envelopes, stamps, or blank cards). Publications received with C/Ds, DVDs, or Blue Ray discs will result in the entire publication being returned to the sender, though some spots will tear out the discs and send the book to the cellblock. Free gifts included in book orders will be returned to the sender. Hobby craft items may not be received in the mail. They must be purchased through commissary.

If something is denied, you should receive a notice from the mailroom stating why. My aunt used to order me books. Occasionally though, I would get a notice from the mailroom letting me know my high-heeled pumps and cocktail dress had been returned to Amazon, when she clicked the wrong address on her Prime Account. Those notices always made me popular at mail call when the guard informed the entire cellblock about my package getting denied.

d. Special Authorization for Incoming Packages

1. Correspondence Courses

You can get special permission to order college classes, vocational training courses, paralegal studies, and personal training certifications. Go to the education department to do this. He or she may give you a special address to avoid the hassle of the mailroom by sending it to an employee mailbox. Incarcerated inmates, thanks to Trump, are now eligible for Pell Grants while in custody.

2. Medical Devices

Most places only allow prescription eyeglasses to be sent like this, but you may get exceptions for hearing aids or dentures. Check with medical.

3. Release Clothing

This will be done through Receiving and Discharge. Ordinarily, you can have pants, a shirt, a belt, socks, shoes, coat, and a travel bag sent to the prison about thirty-days prior to release. Some spots don't do this though. Yazoo city made me leave in my commissary-purchased sweatsuit, but I was so happy to get away from that hellhole, it didn't ruin my day.

e. Normal Incoming Packages

1. Basic Rules

The Bureau permits inmates to subscribe and receive publications without prior approval. The term *publication* refers to a book, single magazine, newspaper, calendar (Without a wire spiral), poster (non-nude), flyer, brochure, or catalog, as long as they are not mass mailed products. Each has to bear the inmate's full name and registration number.

Rules on books vary by institution. Some allow books from any source, even mailed from home. Some will only accept them from a reputable company with the receipt on the package. You just have to investigate local rules when you get there.

Pretty much every spot will refuse any package in bubble wrap, though. Also, materials need to be mailed through the US Postal Service. They're not going to allow a UPS truck to pull up to the front gate with your books or some random person driving for Amazon on-the-side. Don't order more than five books at a time, or they will be refused. Though, Leavenworth allowed six.

2. Prohibited Material

The warden will reject a publication if it is determined to be detrimental to the security, good order, or discipline of the institution, or if it might facilitate criminal activity.

The following publications will be rejected:

- Describes procedures for the construction or use of weapons, ammunition, bombs, or incendiary devices. Having said that, I've seen *Guns and Ammo* inside a few prisons, not all.
- It describes methods of escape from correctional facilities or contains blueprints, drawings, or similar descriptions of Federal Bureau of Prisons' institutions. (Some facilities have banned simple, narrative non-fiction, like *The Hothouse: Life at Leavenworth Prison*.
- It depicts or describes procedures for the brewing of alcoholic beverages or the manufacture of drugs. (My buddy got an incident report or (shot) for having a copy of *Mad Dog's Prison Cookbook*, because it had a recipe for hooch.)
- It is written in code.
- It encourages activities which may lead to use of physical violence or group disruption. (This is supposed to stop racist material too, but I know plenty of inmates who received the Nation of Islam's newspaper, *The Final Call*, and white racists usually have copies of *The Turner Diaries*, and *The Silent Brotherhood*. For this stuff, it really depends on how vigilant mailroom workers do their jobs.)
- It encourages or instructs the commission of criminal activity. (*The Anarchist's Cookbook* and almost every book Paladin Press publishes has been banned. They don't even allow the catalogs in anymore.)
- It is sexually explicit, or features nudity. Porn is banned. With the

availability of smart phones now, most of the old scams for acquiring porn have phased out; however, one of your homies might have his wife order you a fireman or cowboy calendar with dudes with their shirts off though, just for a laugh at mail call.

A WORD OF WARNING

Sex offenders get extra scrutiny in this regard. I've seen pedophiles get sent to the SO Program, and threatened new charges or civil commitment, just for having innocent photos of children clipped from magazines.

A WORD OF WARNING TO NON—SEX OFFENDERS

Keep in mind, if you rent a cell phone in the cellblock, chomos also might have used it to look up smut. If that phone is captured, everyone who handled could potentially catch a sex case, whether they rented it for kiddie porn or not. Any numbers on a smart phone that also exist on a TRULINC'S account result in an easy conviction.

f. New Rules Due to Drug Use

Prisons have banned greeting cards and card stock, because smugglers spray them with K-2 or other drugs. For similar reasons, some places have banned hardback books. In the strictest settings, inmates receive photocopies of all mail, even photographs. You just have to see how anal staff are where you end up.

My buddy, Chance (Yeah, his mama took one), had a friend buy books from a local store. He would take them home, slice open the hardbacks, and fill them with tobacco. After sealing the novels, he returned them to the store and paid the employee to send the package to the prison. Chance caught a new case when they figured out what he was doing. They can bring contraband charges for stuff that isn't normally an illegal substance, like tobacco, phones, alcohol, clothes, shoes, weightlifting supplements, or anything else convicts crave.

g. Special Mail

1. Outgoing

Special mail is a category of correspondence which may be sent out of the institution unopened and unread by staff. This feature only matters at mediums and pens, because all outgoing mail can be sealed in the lower-security facilities. Mail that qualifies for this privilege includes legal correspondence, anything going to the military (for veterans), or any governmental entity.

Inmates needed take advantage of this privilege or to the mailroom posted open house hours with the letter.

2. Incoming

Special mail has to be opened in the inmate' s presence. They only are allowed to check the package to verify it's special (e.g., legal mail or from a government entity). They also search for contraband, but they are not allowed to read the document' s contents. The mail needs to be labeled, *legal mail*, or clearly indicates special mail status. Otherwise, it will be handled as general mail.

h. Inmate Correspondence with Representatives of the News Media

An inmate may use Special Mail Outgoing writing procedures to communicate with members of the news media. The letter must specify name, title, and organization. The inmate may not receive compensation or anything of value for correspondence with the news media. The inmate may not act as a reporter, published under a byline, or conduct a business or profession while in Bureau custody.

Representatives of the news media may initiate correspondence with an inmate. Correspondence from a representative of the news media will be opened when it enters the prison and be treated as general correspondence.

i. Correspondence Between Confined Inmates

An inmate may be permitted to correspond with a prisoner confined in another penal or correctional institution. This is permitted if the other inmate is either a member of the immediate family, or is a party in an *ongoing* legal action (or witness) in which other parties are involved. You will have to show your counselor proof to meet the criteria for the latter option.

My codefendant and I wrote to one another throughout our entire direct-appeals process. They cut us off after our Writ of Certiorari got denied. These days, guys with permission can use snail mail, or they can email each other on the TRULINCS system. Your counselor will handle the approval/rejection process.

You also can get permission to write family in state or municipal custody. There will be a few more hurdles to jump through, though. It took my friend almost six months to clear all the red tape to write his son in a North Carolina state-run facility.

K. Basic Daily Procedure

1. Call Out/Change Sheet
  I. Call Out

This sheet lists every inmate appointment for the following day. The Call-Out Sheet is released at 2:00 PM each afternoon. There should be a hardcopy version and another posted on the TRULINCS Bulletin Board. Make sure you check the Call Out every day. If you miss an appointment, you could face a possible incident report.

This is how medical, psychology, education, Unit Team, the chapel, and every other department schedules you into their rotation. Besides getting in trouble, you might miss out on an opportunity you want. For instance, if you forget a dental-hygienist appointment, you might not get rescheduled for a cleaning for months or years.

  II. Change Sheet

The Change Sheet is at the back of every Call Out Sheet. This lists inmate moves for the day, to another housing unit, cell change, off the compound (hospital, court, or transfers to another prison), or anyone getting sent to the hole/SHU. It also lists changes in work assignments to a new department or from *Unassigned* to your first job.

2. Movements

I. Camps

This one doesn't apply to minimum-security, where inmates are labeled "Out Custody," not required to be housed behind the fence, and can pretty much move anywhere on the prison grounds except during a count, emergency lockdown, or after a certain time each night. Stricter procedures exist behind the razor wire. There, movement is restricted on the compound.

  II. Lows

Those usually have ten-minute moves every hour on the hour. When the public-address system announces the move, the exits to all the compound's buildings are opened (unfortunately, not the front gate). Inmates have ten minutes to walk from the cellblocks to: recreation, education, the chapel, medical, or back from these areas to the housing units.

When I first came into the system, many lows had open compounds, like camps, at least part of the day, and the entire day on weekends or holidays. Unfortunately, staff always tighten rules, nearly never the reverse. Now more lows are run like mediums than camps.

III. Mediums

Some mediums have ten-minute moves. Some have five-minute *incoming* moves. Once every inmate clears the compound, they call a five-minute *outgoing* move from the cellblocks. Some mediums break them down even further, calling out bound moves by cellblock. It's all meant to heighten control. A lot of mediums have divided yards like are described in the next section.

IV. Penitentiaries

These use the most restrictive movement system. Inmates may be forced only interact with prisoners in their cellblocks. The rest of the general population never intermingles. Each cellblock will have a special move and assigned time to go to the chapel, recreation, or education. They hope to decrease violence by reducing the times convicts cross each other's paths.

3. Counts

a. Standing Counts

One of the realities of institutional life is counts. During official counts, cell doors will be locked at mediums and pens. Some lows have cells as well, but in the lower securities, no doors are locked. In a dormitory setting, inmates have to stand beside their beds.

Standing counts take place system-wide at 4:00 PM and 10:00 PM every day, as well as 10:00 AM counts on weekends and holidays. The 10:00 PM standing count was added about halfway into my sentence. Before that, you could be asleep in your bunk when they came around at 10:00 PM.

They changed that rule after an inmate in a pen killed his cellie. Afterwards, he played *Weekend at Bernie's* with the body during the next day's 4:00 PM standing count. Almost every new rule or change in policy came from an inmate doing something like this or worse.

When a count is announced, inmates have to go to their cells or living quarters. At mediums and pens, you will be locked in your cell at 4:00 PM, 10:00 PM, and 10:00 AM (on weekends) until the count clears. This usually takes sixty to ninety minutes. Most guys use this period to take a nap or go to sleep for the night.

In higher securities, you'll stay locked in your cell after the 10:00 PM count until around 5:30 to 6:00 AM the next morning. Lows and campers can return to TV rooms and common areas after the 10:00 PM count clears, but they will be locked in the cellblock/housing unit until breakfast the next morning.

I actually missed the nightly lockdowns when I went down in security. I always went to sleep after the 10:00 PM count and woke at 5:30 AM. In some lows inmates stay up all night. They are loud, obnoxious and don't show as much respect as they would in a more violent prison. If you're a light sleeper at a low, you may need to become a night owl and lie down when the guys in your cut do.

Make sure you're fully dressed when they count. A female guard might write you a shot if you don't have a shirt on, even in your cell with the door closed and locked. Don't talk, and depending on how strict the place, you may not want to wear headphones. I once had to do extra duty, because I wasn't facing an asshole guard when he counted (The inmate version of chores to avoid further punishment).

b. Non-Standing Late-Night Counts

They conduct these counts every night at 12:00 AM, 3:00 AM, and 5:00 AM to make sure you haven't tunneled through the cement and rebar. In the higher securities, you will be locked in your cell and probably asleep, at least until you take a flashlight beam to the face, anyway.

Like Pavlov's dog, I was programmed to wake up and empty my bladder around 3:00 AM every night. Sometimes, I would be at the toilet when the light came. If that happens to you, try not to spray the wall as you try to put it away before a female guard starts screaming at you. Other times, they woke me with their laughter, loud conversation, and rattling keys.

Earplugs help with that. If your commissary doesn't sell them, you can buy them from an inmate who works in the facilities building or at Unicor. To fight the bright light on your eyelids, pull a knit hat down low or make a facemask. Don't pull the blanket over your head though, or they'll kick your door until you move. That's a good way to piss off your cellie.

c. Census Counts

1. General Census Counts

Inmates call these "Sense-less" counts. Some spots don't do them. Some guards refuse to waste their time with them even on compounds that order them. If they occur, they will take place, Monday-Friday, in the morning after work call, sometime between 8:00 AM-9:00 AM. If it happens again, it will be between 12:30 PM-1:00 PM in the afternoon.

You won't be locked in your cell for this. Your unit guard will walk around with a clipboard and ask your name. It usually takes twenty minutes to clear. You can avoid these by leaving the building in the morning or early afternoon. Just go to recreation, the chapel, or education. If you have a job outside the cellblock, you will avoid them also.

2. Locked-Down Census Counts

These are surprise counts weekdays to catch inmates out-of-bounds. Mostly, they are meant to surprise housing-unit orderlies who are outside exercising or shooting pool instead of doing their jobs in the cellblock. Depending on the prison, if you get caught somewhere you're not supposed to be, you could get an incident report, lose your job, and/or go to the hole. To avoid trouble when you have an orderly job, ask the unit guard if it's okay to leave the building. Guys skipping classes and call-outs can be considered *out-of-bounds* too.

d. Emergency Counts

Prison staff love to count. Anytime there is a lockdown over an emergency, a standing count will follow afterwards. They do these when the touch sensors go out on the perimeter fence (at least once a month), or the cameras or radios stop working. They do them for reduced visibility: heavy rain, thunderstorms, fog, or white-out snow conditions. After any group protests, serious violence, large-scale brawls, racial tension, a count follows the lockdown.

Part Six: First, Three-Months in Custody

A. The Administration and Orientation Program (A&O)

An orientation program normally gets scheduled within a couple months of arriving at a facility. All new commitments and those who return to the institution after an absence of more than ninety days have to complete the program. Your prison will give you a handbook covering much of what *First 90* discusses when you go to A&O, but I find it to be too little too late for new fish.

If A&O starts sixty days after arrival, you've already discovered much of it on your own. I wrote this book to help my readers avoid the time lag and difficult learning curve most new fish endure. By reading this book, you already will know everything covered in the seminar, plus more.

The A&O coordinator handles most of the presentation, but department heads from every prison office will be called in to talk about and answer questions concerning their area of expertise. A&O usually wraps up in one day. I've never seen one take longer than two.

Since you already know most of the material covered, the seminar really will only matter to you in two ways. First, they have some forms for you to fill out:

- Acknowledgment Form (Did you receive them all?)
- Uniform Basic Safety Regulations
- Hazard Communication
- Institution's Policy on Illegal Substances
- Accident Compensation
- Education/Recreation Needs Assessments

The forms have to be filled out, and A&O otherwise completed, before you are allowed to get a job. This is important for guys who need to earn a living inside. It also is important to men who don't want to work while in custody. I'll explain more in the next section.

B. Job Assignment

1. How to Avoid a Job

Inmates have to maintain a job in most prisons. A few facilities don't enforce this rule though, Leavenworth for one. Covid protocol relaxed this too. Just ask around where you land. If you end up somewhere that doesn't care, and don't feel like hustling for the man, you can do other things to enjoy your newfound abundance of leisure time.

You still have options even on a mandatory-work yard. If you have a physical or mental disability, a serious illness, or are a senior citizen, you can ask a doctor to medically-exempt you from an assignment at the prison. If you are self-surrendering, get a note from your street doctor.

Otherwise, get a *sign-in job*. Yards have more inmates than meaningful work. The paint shop guard might have spots for ten workers but twenty-five slots on his roster. The extra fifteen won't get paid or ever pick up a bucket or brush. At the morning work call, the non-workers will walk to the boss's office to sign the roster sheet. Then, they can do what they want.

If you don't get a medical exemption, sign-in job, or find an assignment you actually want, you could end up on the morning's kitchen crew, waking at 3:30 AM to go to the chow hall to do something stupid, like roll napkins around plastic sporks.

2. Finding the Right Job

You won't be able to get a job before you complete A&O. Ask your homies with good work assignments if they can get you on their work crew. You always can find another inmate who is tight with his boss. Homies call these inmates "*suck*-cretaries" one of the guys in your car should be able to hook you up with the job.

If you have special trade skills, you can approach a guard at facilities to get on the HVAC, carpentry, landscaping, welding, painting, electrical, or plumbing crew. Inmates with higher education can be law clerks, tutors, or teach, *Adult Continuing Education (ACE)* classes.

To avoid an unfavorable assignment thrust on you by your counselor, find somewhere you want to work. Talk to the guard over the section. Ask him or her to sign a Cop-Out agreeing to hire you, and take it to your counselor to be added to the Change Sheet.

3. Inmate Performance Pay System (IPPS)

This is the pay scale for jobs in the system. (Subject to change at any time)

- Grade 4 = $0.12 per hour
- Grade 3 = $0.17 per hour
- Grade 2 = $0.29 per hour
- Grade 1 = $0.40 per hour

Typically, guys start at *maintenance pay*, $5.25 per month. As they acquire specific assignments, they work up the grade scale. Usually, each work section only has one or two *Grade 1* workers. In addition to pay grades, inmates can earn up to 50% bonus on their monthly pay, many years of budget cuts have decreased how many guys get these now.

Failure to pay fines (*FRP-Refusal*) and other monetary obligations, or failure to participate in required drug education, or to show progress toward educational goals will result in pay restrictions. You need either a diploma, GED, or be enrolled in a GED class to earn *any* pay grade.

4. Unicor (Prison Industries)

a. What Is It?

These are the best jobs available if you want to send money home to your kids or save some for release. A Unicor job also makes them stop hounding you about fines or restitution. They simply confiscate half your wages to pay off your debts. Unfortunately, the FBOP has been phasing out the program over the past decade.

Unicor factories perform various services and produce many products (e.g., clothes, chairs, print services, recycling, and much more) most for the military and prison system. Since they don't have to compete for government contracts, and they have unlimited slave labor available, many business owners in the public-sector would like to see Unicor disbanded.

b. Waiting Lists

*If you want to get into Unicor more quickly, talk to your counselor about getting on a waiting list as soon as you arrive. *

Unicor uses four waiting lists for inmates wanting a job:

1. Previous Unicor employment. If you transfer to a new spot and worked at Unicor at your last prison, you get top priority.

2. Financial Obligations (FRP). If you owe money, you get second priority, only below the guys with prior experience.

3. Twenty-four Months List. If an inmate has two years or less left on their sentences, they get the third priority, because they may need to save money before release, and Unicor will have to pay them as much since they don't have time to earn Grades or Longevities.

4. General List. No debt, no prior, long sentence, but still wants to work.

They pick a couple from each list when they hire inmates, but the higher lists are faster to cycle through.

c. Unicor Pay Scale

- Grade 5 = $0.23 per hour
- Grade 4 = $0.46 per hour
- Grade 3 = $0.69 per hour
- Grade 2 = $0.92 per hour
- Grade 1 = $1.15 per hour

Inmates cannot go above a Grade 4 without a diploma or GED. The education part verified. Overtones computed on a double basis. (My cellie averaged eighty plus hours per week at FCI-Petersburg's print shop.) To receive overtime pay, you first completed the total hours of the day which will be worked.

d. Unicor Longevity Payouts

Inmates who work a certain number of months at Unicor will be eligible for these pay increases:

- eighteen months = $0.10 per hour
- thirty months = $0.15 per hour
- forty-two months = $0.20 per hour
- sixty months = $0.25 per hour
- eighty-four months = $0.30 per hour

C. How Much Time You Actually Have to Do

1. Good Time for Every Inmate

This applies to every inmate, without life, sentenced for an offense committed after November 1, 1987 (The day federal parole ended. Thanks, Joe Biden!) when the Comprehensive Crime Control Act became law. The two most significant changes in the sentencing statutes deal with good time and parole. Parole no longer exists. The only good time available under this law is fifty-four days.

For years, there was a discrepancy where inmates were losing seven days per year in the way the Bureau tabulated good time. A provision in the First Step Act 2018 fixed it. Seven days may not seem like much, but it added a six-month reduction in my case.

This minor cut basically means you do 85% of a court-imposed sentence, you stay out of trouble. I managed to get through my sentence with only one shot for the eighty-man brawl I mentioned earlier. I lost twenty-seven good days for getting my ass kicked.

2. First Step Time Cut

FIRST Step-eligible inmates can earn one year off their sentence. It just takes a little longer for some to earn it than others. I discussed this earlier. It depends on PATTERN Score whether you will earn five, ten, or fifteen days for every thirty days of programming.

3. RDAP-Year Reduction

I already covered the Residential Drug Abuse Program earlier. Completing the course gives eligible inmates a year off their sentences. To be awarded the time cut, you can't have a gun charge, sex crime involving actual contact, or any violence. Also, you have to mention your drug or alcohol problem during your Pre-Sentence Interview.

In addition, you are guaranteed to get at least four months in a Residential Reentry Facility (Halfway House). Graduates have to continue treatment for 120 days in a community, near release facility. This ensures each eligible participant will leave prison at least sixteen months before his sentence is scheduled to end.

4. Residential Reentry Centers

Between the *Second Chance Act* and the *First Step Act*, inmates can earn up to one year in a halfway house or on home confinement. This is in addition to any other accrued good time.

5. Problems with Getting Every Time Cut

The main problem for guys with sentences five years or less is that they will run out of sentence before they earn every cut. For example, if an inmate has a sixty-month sentence, and is eligible for everything, this is how it will play out:

- He automatically gets fifty-four days off per year, for a total of 230 days. This leaves four years, four months, and fifteen days.
- If the inmate self-surrenders, he'll have all the remaining time to work, but if he was denied bail, he will spend at least six months in county jail or a holding center before going to prison. It will be six wasted months where he won't be able to earn as much as fifteen days per

month off his sentence for programming under the *First Step Act*.

- Completing RDAP will reduce the sentence by sixteen months, leaving three years and two weeks left.

- Inmates have to program to earn the year off under the *First Step Act*. In the best of circumstances, they earn fifteen days per month, taking two years to get full time credit. Those in the lowest category earn five days each month, taking six years to earn it all.

- Factor in that he automatically will be eligible for six months in a halfway house or on home confinement, you can see the limit for some guys to earn everything. Considering most people get sentenced to sixty months or less, the vast majority in the FBOP will not get everything. Congress intended this when they originally passed the good-time laws.

D. Medical Services

1. Sick Call

Every facility does *Sick Call* a little differently. Covid changed long-used procedures almost everywhere too. Usually, sick call is held after breakfast on Monday, Tuesday, Thursday, and Friday. Wednesdays are reserved for A&O initial screenings: Physicals, dental checks, and required lab tests. If you need treatment when you first arrive, bring the issues up in the screening process. The main purpose of lab work is clear you to work in food services. They test for TB, HIV, and Hep-C.

If your facility holds sick call the most popular way, you show up for triage in the morning. A nurse will write down your symptoms or ailments and schedule a time for you to see someone higher up the food chain at a later time. If the issue is serious, and they aren't busy, they will treat you then. Prisons that have stopped in-person sick call due to the pandemic will give you a sick call form to fill out or tell you to send medical an email via TRULINCS.

2. Co-Pay

You have to pay $2.00 every time you visit, Sick Call. The FBOP did this to help offset costs, but also to stop frivolous complaints. Many lonely inmates develop hypochondria and seek emotional validation from medical staff. (You'll be shocked to see how many guys who can walk are getting pushed around in wheelchairs at your facility.)

Also, predators use Sick Call as a way to expose themselves to staff without catching a new case. Testicular hernias or prostate exams are used as a ploy to drop their pants in front of females, and even the male staff.

You will pay two dollars every time you initiate a medical visit; however, if the doctor puts you on call out for follow-up treatment, you will not be charged.

This experience will give you a glimpse of what free, government healthcare would look like: long waits, poor service, automatic refusal for any and all cutting-edge treatment, and poor service. Ibuprofen 800s being the only help a person can expect around 70% of the time.

3. Chronic Care

Chronic Care is a designation inmates, who need long-term treatment, get. Staff call them in for regular exams and lab work, in addition to any treatment their diseases, handicaps, or injuries require. They are not charged a co-pay when staff initiate the visit.

4. Care Levels

Each federal prison is ranked one through four. *One* represents a prison that is more than an hour from an outside hospital. A *Two* is a prison that is less than an hour from an outside hospital. A *Three* is on a compound with a prison hospital located on the grounds. A *Four* is a Federal Medical Center (FMC), a prison hospital. There are seven *Fours* in the FBOP:

- FMC Butner, North Carolina
- FMC Devens, Massachusetts
- FMC Rochester, Minnesota
- FMC Carswell, Texas (Female)
- FMC Lexington, Kentucky (Low Custody)
- MCFP Springfield, Missouri (High Security)
- FMC Fort Worth, Texas

5. Over-the-Counter Medications (OTCS)

Over-the-counter medications are supposed to be purchased through commissary. Indigent inmates have to submit OTC medication requests to the institution's pharmacy. Chronic care inmates also receive some over-the-counter medication along with their other prescriptions.

Try to keep your locker stocked with any medication you might need if you catch a cold, contract an upset stomach, have heartburn, or feel any other ailment you often have. Nothing sucks worse than having a sore throat, and your next commissary shopping opportunity is six days away. Plus, you never know when you will get caught in an extended lockdown with no store. Some prisons allow sick inmates to buy meds anytime commissary is open, but you'll be much happier if the stuff is in your locker when you need it.

Some cool doctors will prescribe you Ibuprofen 800s, antacids, laxatives, and other basic stuff, even if you aren't indigent, but it really depends on the attitudes of the employees at medical at your prison. Ask your homies. They will know whether it will be worth the effort to go to sick call for free OTCs.

6. Prescriptions

Some medications are given to patients all at once. They only do this when there is no risk of overdose or abuse. When a doctor writes a prescription, you can usually pick it up that day at the next pill line.

If the drug is something you need to take continually, TRULINCS has a feature you can click on when you need a refill. After logging on, go to pill line and pick up the drug.

7. Pill/Insulin Line Procedures

Many medicines are banned in the FBOP (e.g., opioids, Xanax, except for hospitalized inmates), and no personal medicines may be sent into a facility or brought from home, even upon the advice of a doctor. Every prison has its own pharmacy. Your initial screening will determine your needs. Staff will prescribe new medications after you arrive.

Medications that are not given out in full scripts (e.g., Neurontin, insulin, etc.) Have to be picked up in daily doses at the pill line window. Normally, pill line runs before breakfast and dinner. This allows diabetics to eat as soon as they take their shots.

Any medication an inmate might be tempted to abuse will be crushed before being handed out. The pharmacist will splash the powder with an ounce or two of water and demand it be taken immediately. The staff member will then check the prisoner's mouth to make sure it was swallowed.

Convicts still manage to hide the paste between cheek and gums. They leave the window and spit the drug in a tissue. Believe it or not, there's a black market for all pills that create anything resembling a buzz. I wouldn't be surprised if some cons just open their beaks like a baby bird and wait for their dealer to hawk it up. Needless to say, hepatitis C and worse, afflicts many addicted inmates.

You will be required to show your prison identification card every time you go to pill line. Although inmates are not forced to take any pill line medication or insulin, if they previously agreed to the treatment, they have to report to pill line. If they don't show up, they will receive an incident report. If they want to get off the medication, they have to sign a refusal form at medical. This indemnifies the Bureau against a lawsuit, if a refusal leads to worse health or death.

8. Medical Emergencies

If you have a medical emergency, approach the nearest staff member. That employee will contact the *on-call* medical person. They always have someone on hand, even late at night and on weekends. If your cell is locked, there is a panic button near the door. Push it and scream the *Life Alert* catchphrase.

Unfortunately, the quality of care you get depends on who is on staff at the time. Normally, an inmate in cardiac arrest will die during the thirty minutes or so it takes to clear red tape and put him in an ambulance. I've seen it happen a lot.

My friend at FCI-Beckley complained to the guard in his cellblock about a massive headache behind his right eyeball. It was Monday night when the CO called medical. The nurse on staff refused to examine him or check his vitals. He told the guard to tell the inmate to report to sick call in the morning. My buddy had an aneurysm and died at the guard's feet a few minutes later.

A guy in my housing unit at FCI-Petersburg had a stroke on a Friday night. The entire left side of his face was paralyzed, but they still refused to even look at him until Monday morning. Then, they didn't take him to the outside hospital until Thursday. Luckily, it was a minor stroke. He was in pretty good health and only fifty at the time. He made a full recovery, no thanks to prison medical staff.

My advice: *Take care of yourself in there, physically, mentally, and spiritually. Become proactive concerning your own well-being.* Volume IV in this series: *Doing Time the Right Way*, explains the things I did to survive incarceration for twenty-three years and leave the place in fantastic health. Volume III in the series is offered for free on my website:www.fromcell2soul.com[1]: *A Meaningful Life Requires a Meaningful Effort.*

---

9. Specialists

If the doctor or physician's assistant can't offer sufficient treatment, specialists will be consulted. Generally, every *Care Level II* facility contracts with a surgeon, orthopedic, optometrist, or other specialist. They come to the prison every now and again to treat patients. Inmates also are taken to local clinics and hospitals to receive special treatment the prison can't provide. At *Care Level III* and *Care Level IV* facilities the specialists are on site on the compound.

Certain treatments are banned though. Don't expect to get experimental cutting-edge treatment. You won't see a chiropractor, natural medical practitioner, pain doctor, nutritionist, or physical therapist. If an inmate has a chronic illness he or she could be sent to the Federal Medical Center (Care Level IV-A Prison Hospital).

10. What to Do if You Have Problems Receiving Treatment

This is a big problem and requires more instruction than I can fit into this introductory book. I will cover it in detail in Part III: *Navigating the Federal Bureau of Prisons' Regulations, Procedures, and Rules*. Having said that, let me give you a few tips here:

a. Be Persistent

Staff are trained to spin inmates (All of them, not just medical staff) because of all the frivolous complaints. Keep going back to *sick call*. Explain how bad you feel, and never lose your temper, no matter how disrespectful or unhelpful they are.

b. Get Started on the Process Immediately

Guys with torn ACLs usually wait twenty-four months for surgery. So don't put off going to medical. Go to sick call as soon as it happens. If you have a short sentence, they will try to make you wait till release for non-life-saving surgery. Start early. Keep returning to sick call, and force them to act.

c. Start the Administrative Remedy Process

Step-by-step instructions of this process will be covered in *Volume 3*. For now, you can get the ball rolling by filing a *BP-8* (Don't do this unless they are being uncooperative and refusing to help.) Your counselor handles this when you file. Just make it clear you have a serious health issue, that you are dealing with a lot of pain, and all you want is adequate treatment. The *BP-8* is only the first step in the process, but sometimes it is enough. If medical still doesn't want to help, you can continue this filing process to completion. It usually takes around eighteen months, and it paves the way for a lawsuit in federal court, if it becomes necessary.

d. Get Your Congressperson Involved

If the paperwork doesn't feel like it's helping, have a family member contact his or her local representative. This is such a common problem, most congresspeople have a staff member assigned to handle these complaints. Just make sure the issue is serious. If you do it over a frivolous complaint, you'll burn through the elected official's goodwill pretty fast.

The congressperson will need your written permission to get involved and review your medical files. Someone from medical will call you down to sign some release forms, granting permission for the congressperson's people to see your medical files. Involving outside help like this will anger the prison's administration, but it may be your only way to get treatment when you need it.

11. Routine Physical Examinations

You will have a routine exam and lab done soon after you arrive. They will test your blood in order to clear you for a potential job in food service. You can't work in the dining hall with any contagious disease that might put the general population at risk.

Inmates under the age of fifty may request a periodic health examination every three years from the last one. Older inmates and chronic-care patients will be examined at least every six months but most likely more often. Inmates close to being released from custody may request a physical examination, if they haven't had one within one year of their release date.

They will check your prostate if you submit a request. Some guys ask a for second, and even a third, opinion. Just make sure the doctor doesn't put both hands on your shoulders when he probes you!

12. Dental Sick Call

This occurs at the same time as regular sick call. They will fill cavities or pull teeth. They won't do root canals, bridgework, or crowns. They *will* provide dentures to inmates who don't have enough teeth to properly digest their food, but expect a long wait. So, if you need dentures, start the process as soon as you arrive!

Some prisons have terrible dentists who try to get away with no treatment other than pulling teeth, and I've heard horror stories of them breaking surrounding teeth as they pulled the bad one. Refusing to save a tooth that can be saved is illegal. They have to put a filling in any tooth not too far gone, but you may have to push paperwork.

13. Routine Dental Care

There is usually a two-year waiting list to see a hygienist. So, sign up for a dental cleaning as soon as you arrive at your prison. Send an email via TRULINCS. If you don't get a response, send a paper cop-out to the hygienist. The waiting list is a national one. So, if you get transferred before the cleaning, you don't have to go to the bottom of the list at your new compound.

Following the cleaning, you will be x-rayed and seen by the dentist. If you have any cavities, you will be scheduled for them to be filled at a future date. That's the best-case scenario anyway. The dentist at FCI-Petersburg would only use temporary fillings, and it usually took six trips to dental, sick call before she would actually do the work. Honestly, she left a molar in worse shape than when I first entered her office. An initial, simple filling needed a crown when I got out of prison.

There are some good dentists and doctors working for the FBOP, but many finished last in their class in school or have been sued so much on the street they no longer can find a company to provide them malpractice insurance.

There was a rumor that the head doctor at FCI-Petersburg-Low was a former gynecologist who had been sued so many times she could no longer get insurance. I don't know if that was true or not, but she did a good job keeping my Pap smears up to date.

E. Education and Recreation Programs

1. Education Courses

a. Mandatory Courses

All of the following fit the *First Step Act* Program requirements:

a. Literacy Program

ii. *English as a Second Language*
iii. *GED*

These courses are mandatory for the inmates they apply to, until they meet the minimum requirement or earn a GED. Participation meets *First Step Act* programming requirements.

a. Post Secondary Education

1. Vocational Training

These courses and apprenticeship programs are provided by the FBOP. Every facility offers different options. Choice programs often motivate inmates to seek transfers to particular prisons. For instance, years back, FCI-Ashland offered a Harley Davidson, repair certification program. More inmates wanted to take that one than were able to get into it. Some options include:

- Electrical
- HVAC
- Carpentry
- Welding
- Masonry
- Machining
- Culinary Arts
- Plumbing
- Hospitality Services

- Basic Computer Skills
- Green Awareness
- Major Appliance Repair
- Small Engine Repair
- Drafting
- Dental/X-ray Tech
- Unicor-Related, Factory-Based Skills

The guy who ran the VT Program at FCI-Beckley taught every phase of home construction. He even had a small home inmates rebuilt over and over in the warehouse on the compound. Even more amazing, the shop teacher still had all his fingers.

2. College

Some prisons contract with local, junior colleges for professors who enter the prison. Bluefield State used to teach basic elective-type courses at FCI-Beckley. Prisoners could not earn a degree, but they could earn around twenty-one hours in transferable credit.

3. Correspondence Courses

These courses aren't free. You have to pay for them, and if the schools require proof against cheating, the education department will provide one for testing. I finished my degree through Ohio University like this. Unfortunately, the classes cost over a thousand bucks each (for three, credit hours), but there's good news to combat costs. I'll explain in the next section.

4. Adult Continuing Education (ACE)

These classes are designed and taught by inmates. You won't get First Step Credit, but FCI-Beckley had a tenured professor from Yale teaching physics. My Spanish teacher spoke four languages and use to work for the State Department. Bernie Madoff taught pyramid-scheme maintenance at FCI-Butner, *just kidding*, but there are a lot of highly, educated professionals in there. They also are as bored as everyone else. Teaching ACE courses helps them pass the time.

c. Pell Grants

The last piece of legislation Trump signed into law, the CARES Act, opened Pell grants to inmates while they are incarcerated. It went into effect in July of 2023. Either go to the education department at your prison or have your family go to FAFSA.gov and print off a copy of the application for you. You may not qualify, if you already hold a degree, but it can't hurt to apply and see if you can fund some college classes or other programs while you are incarcerated.

2. Recreation

a. Leagues

If you are inclined athletically, sign up for a sports team. There's no better way to make time pass. Facilities provide a wide range of choices. Softball usually is the most popular, but you can find basketball, volleyball, soccer, Ultimate Frisbee, flag football and for some sports, they do A (Greater Skill) and B Leagues, as well as one for guys forty and over.

a. Classes

1. First Step Approved

These recreation-sponsored classes will grant the added benefit of the good time available to eligible inmates.

1. Inmate Led Classes

i. Wellness

These might not earn the extra good time, but they will get you in shape, provide something to look forward to each day, help time pass more quickly, and aid sleep at night. Options usually include: Yoga (I taught this my whole bit.), Calisthenics, or Core-Fit, Insanity, Spin, and they usually do something for beginners, the overweight, and/or older inmates.

ii. Hobby Skills Classes

If you already have artistic skills, have taken a hobby craft class and want to continue, sign up for a locker at recreation. Classes provide materials free of charge to help you learn, but after that you have to purchase tools, almost all materials out of pocket. Having said that, once you develop some skills, other convicts will hound you to make stuff for them. Many guys support themselves selling their artwork.

c. Other Ways the Recreation Department can Help You Bid

1. Independent Wellness Activities

Every facility has equipment like: stationary bikes, treadmills, ellipticals, and such. They provide exercise mats, yoga mats, ab wheels, jump ropes, medicine balls, and foam rollers. Some facilities also provide instructional DVDs on various health aspects. Beyond that, it will depend where you are.

Every facility built post-1995 won't have a weight pile or any equipment to build muscle. You can thank former Congressman Dick Zimmer for these changes. In that year, he proposed a bill that banned pornography, R-rated movies, training in martial arts, weightlifting equipment, coffee pots in cells, pay-per-view fights, and weightlifting supplements. The bill never became law, but the Federal Bureau of Prisons still implemented every aspect of the law into their policy. This is why some facilities have super-strict policies about training upper-body strength. In the craziest ones, you may get a write-up if they catch you doing pull-ups or dips

I am an American Council on Exercise (ACE) certified personal trainer. I've taught yoga for over twenty years. I also have over two-decades experience creating jerry-rigged workouts in federal prison with scarce equipment. Volume IV, in my *Doing Time the Right Way* series, will show you how to get felon fit and build strength without weights.

Most health-conscious inmates try to get to yards with a weight pile. There are still a few built before 1995 that have them. The lows and camps have the most options, but the new policy is that weights can't be repaired or replaced. They get thrown in the trash as dumbbells and bars bust.

Dropping the fragile, rusted equipment to the ground from waist height is a good way to get beat up. Treat the equipment with care. Set it down gently, and explain the protocol to new fish who work out with you.

2. Miscellaneous Activities

Rec also provides ping-pong tables, pool tables (Unless, guys have used the sticks and balls in a brawl.), bocce pits, or horse shoes, corn toss, (Yes, it's corn *toss*. In prison, corn *holing* means something you probably want to avoid.), and/or board games. You can check out musical instruments and even purchase your own harmonicas. Several musicians can form a band and get assigned time in a room with a PA and speakers (no electric guitars though), but bands have to play for gen pop every three months or may lose their slot.

F. Religious Services

1. Options

Most facilities offer services for: Protestants, Catholics (Usually, there is one is available in English and Spanish), Sunni Islam, Buddhism, Hinduism, Santería, Native American, Asatru/Odinism, Jehovah's Witnesses, Seven Day Adventists, Nation of Islam, Moorish Science Temple, House of Yahweh, and Wicca. If you practice something else, you can get a time slot by filling out a *BP-S822* form. *Volume III: Navigating the Federal Bureau of Prisons' Regulations, Rules, and Procedures*, will show you what to do to force a stubborn chaplain to do his or her job.

Most chaplains are Christian and extremely hostile to all other faiths. Some make insulting comments about other belief systems. Others drag their feet on every legitimate request you make.

I had to file paperwork for a year straight, and then, threaten a Biven's Lawsuit, before FCI-Beckley's chaplain allowed my Taoist group to worship and receive a budget for materials. I encountered the same resistance when I transferred to USP Leavenworth. The chaplain there gave me a timeslot immediately, but not before calling me an idiot for my beliefs. Then, he told the guys, I was teaching beginner's meditation to, that they were going to hell, if they didn't stop.

2. Chapel Time

Most groups get one slot per week. Christians always receive more time and resources. If your group is small, it will be inmate led. Larger groups have volunteers coming from the street to lead services. Chaplains oversee their personal faith groups. These mostly will be Protestants, but there are few Muslims, Jews, and Catholic priests who worked for the FBOP.

Small groups may get occasional faith leaders from the community, maybe a couple times a year. If you know a potential volunteer, do not contact the person yourself. That would kill any chance the man or woman would be allowed inside the prison. Instead, hand the chaplain a list of potential faith groups near your prison. Put your favorite at the top.

3. Budgets

Every group gets an annual budget to buy materials. The larger the group, the more money. Chapels usually have libraries already stocked with books and audio/visual materials all from previous budgets or donations. Your allotment can go to more of this or whatever the group needs, like candles, incense, prayer rugs, zafus, zabutons, herbs, and anything else you can prove your faith requires.

My group got extra money, because I proved I needed a particular set of teachings only available in one form. After I filed on the chaplains, they were forced to buy the materials. Filing paperwork like this will be covered thoroughly in *Part III: Navigating the Federal Bureau of Prisons' Rules, Regulations, and Procedures.*

4. Ceremonial Meals

Each group gets one special religious meal per year. This is the best food you eat in prison. Established groups already have the details worked out. Newly appointed faiths need to pick their biggest holiday and inform the chaplain of the date. Plan to get with the chaplain several months before the big day. Most prisons give you a special menu to pick from that the chow hall will provide. Some allow inmates in the religious group to prepare the meal themselves, even if they don't work in the kitchen.

In addition, some chapels provide a budget for additional items not found in the cafeteria. The Native Americans get buffalo meat. Muslims receive dates and other items throughout Ramadan. At the least, no matter the religion, store-bought desserts are provided that you'll never get it any other time during the year

5. Special Purchase Orders (SPOs)

Personal religious items will be provided with chapel funds. Granted, most chapels have pamphlets, brochures, Bibles, Korans, and cheap malas and rosaries for free, but other items have to be ordered from commissary. Prison stores keep prayer oil and kufis in stock too, but special orders usually have to be made for personal prayer rugs, religious medallions, tarot cards, runes, religious headgear, and anything else you can prove you need. You have to use an FBOP-approved vendor and expect commissary to tax you with a 30% hike over retail. They won't let you order live bats though, even if you think Ozzie is the god of rock.

6. Religious Diets

Special diets are available to inmates wanting halal, kosher, vegetarian, or vegan food. In the past, these meals were very nutritious with lots of raw vegetables, and many inmates signed up for the privilege, even if they weren't religiously motivated. To combat misuse, they started serving pre-made, TV dinner-style, meals. If you're doing a long bid, this isn'y a very healthy diet. Plan on supplementing your meals with commissary and contraband chow hall items.

To get on the above diet list, you have to sign up with the chaplain. Some will question you to make sure you can explain your faith requirements. If you are a Buddhist, Hindu (No Beef), or practice something else demanding vegetarianism, you don't need to go to the chapel first. Every meal in the cafeteria has a *no-meat* option. Granted, it's mostly processed soy that looks like it plopped from a can with *Alpo* printed on the side.

Some Muslims and Jews get by on the regular meal plan too. They just skip the few pork meals. Pork chops and bacon disappeared from the national menu many sad, long, years ago.

G. Staying Safe

Staying safe is the main topic covered in Part II: Federal Prison Etiquette (Available at fromcell2soul.com), but I didn't want to finish this introductory book without touching on the subject a little:

1. The Riskiest Behaviors in Federal Prison

Federal Prison can be dangerous even if you do your best to avoid trouble. With that in mind, certain behaviors increase the likelihood you'll experience friction with other inmates. Here's what I consider the top five:

a. Gambling

Almost all the scraps I got into during my first years started during a poker game. I caught guys cheating. Some bottom dealt. Some held cards. I discovered two, Jamaican men passing hands back and forth under the table. Believe it or not, cons even tried to cash in counterfeit poker chips.

Even at honest games, I ran into trouble. Some guys were sore losers. A few refused to pay debts on credit tables.

The game creates tremendous negative energy. Everybody bluffs (lies). Everybody holds bad intentions to take everybody else's money. The game generates greed. On top of that, guys that run tables often are predators, not sexual ones, but they tend to be thirsty and unscrupulous, taking 10% or more of every hand. Many tables belong to gangs, and those guys care about no one but their homies.

Factor the above with the fact that everyone in the game is locked up. Each participant probably already has a lot of frustration and anger simmering. Plus, many guys come into the system with mental issues that make them more prone to violence than the general public.

You're better off staying away from all tables: poker, Tunk, dice, or blackjack. On the other hand, you most likely, won't have trouble if you play parlay tickets. Of course, sports betting odds are extremely skewed in the bookie's favor in prison. Just send me the money you plan on betting instead and at least one of us will be happy.

b. Snitching

Before I get into this, I need to define some prison slang: *Rat* and *jailhouse snitch*. A *rat* is someone who testified on his case for a sentence reduction. This person made enemies of his co-defendants; however, he will file separatees through the FBOP. *Separatees* guarantee he won't face retaliation from any of them, at least until he gets released, because they will never be on the same compound together.

Rats face danger at some medium-security prisons and penitentiaries, but honestly, with conspiracy laws and harsh, mandatory sentences, rats fill every prison these days. The lows and camps have high percentages of them. Rats may be verbally ridiculed, but few will be physically accosted at a minimum-security facility.

On the other hand, *jailhouse snitches* keep the guards informed about what is happening at the prison. *Everyone* dislikes these guys. Some jailhouse snitches didn't even rat on their cases. They might not have known anything juicy enough when they got arrested to squeal on, but some try to put cases on inmates breaking the law while in custody.

Some aren't even looking for a time cut. Those guys just tell them petty stuff, like where a convict hid his plastic bag filled with hooch, out of spite or in hopes the guards will give them some postage stamps (cash in federal prison). Some do it, because they're jealous, assholes with no friends.

Guys *may* not like you if they know you ratted, but they *will* hate you if they know you are snitching on stuff at the prison. Cons have smart phones. Men sell drugs. Others make hooch or shine. If they think you might tell on them, they will become enemies fast.

The safest way through a bit is to develop tunnel vision. Very little privacy exists in federal prison. You will see stuff you shouldn't. Keep it to yourself.

Don't even tell other inmates what you saw. One inmate will tell another. It will continue until a snitch hears and tells a guard. If someone gets busted, and that person knows you saw them breaking the rules, you might be blamed for snitching even if you didn't do it.

c. Using

Drugs create even more problems in prison than the normal ones addiction causes in the free world. Owing debts creates a huge risk and fiends tend to run up bills they can't pay. Some guys resort to locker theft to get out of the hole, and this pretty much guarantees a beating or worse.

Because of the difficulty in obtaining them, drugs come in smaller doses at higher cost in federal facilities, but I've still seen plenty of guys hauled out on a stretcher from heroin and/or fentanyl. You do not want to pass out on dope, drink hooch till you blackout, or go comatose on K-2. An old punchline in the feds is: "Man, I'm never going to smoke deuce again. It always makes my asshole hurt. If you make it a predictable habit, the temptation will be too great for a sexual predator.

d. Screwing

Even if you are a consenting homosexual, you need to be careful. Inmates get possessive over lovers in prison worse than the big drunk dude at a bar with a slutty girlfriend. I've seen brawls start over attractive punks and stabbings over transgenders with breasts.

Beyond that, once predators learn you're gay, they may set sights on you. Typically, effeminate men, transgenders, and young kids get the most attention. Bullies always look for soft targets. They joke, "He might not be gay, but he's just a slap away from it."

Aside from rape, even consensual sex acts are prohibited by policy. You could end up with an incident report, hole time, an unfavorable transfer, and loss of good time. If you do it anyway, you will have no access to condoms, and HIV, Hep C, and more is rampant inside every facility.

e. Owing

This may be an element of *Gambling* and *Using* both, but is important enough to mention again. Usually, the prisoners most likely to fall into debt are junkies and degenerate gamblers. K-2 and Suboxone have hit the federal system hard. The former has an effect on users reminiscent of crack cocaine. It makes fiends willing to steal or do whatever necessary to get high again.

Debtors sometimes accrue bills, and they have to check into protective custody, but this isn't always a solution. Eventually, check-ins leave protective custody. They may get a transfer. They might be forced back onto the same yard.

Don't run up poker debts either. Some store men act as loan sharks to get guys out of immediate trouble, but they charge so much interest, you'll be paying them off for a year.

Don't let guys owe you either. Some hustlers will try to rob you like this. They pick someone not likely to attack them over money, and then borrow stuff with no intention of repaying. Some guys will keep coming back until you show some backbone.

They tend to get more brazen and disrespectful as time goes on. If I didn't hang out with someone, I made a habit of not loaning more than a few dollars to a new person. I used the loan as a test to get a measure of the man. If he paid me back, I stayed open-minded towards friendship. If he didn't, I considered it money well spent to learn the type of guy was. I never pressed those types for money back, but always refused any future request for favors.

This doesn't mean you can't help guys out. You just need to use good judgment. Assist men who deserve it. In those instances, loaning can be an act of kindness with no intention of getting reimbursed.

1. Prison Rape Enforcement Act (PREA)

a. Definition

This Act Passed Congress In 2003. It Defined Sexually Abusive Behavior As:

1. Repeated and unwelcome sexual advances, requests for sexual favors, or verbal comments, gestures, or actions of a derogatory or offensive sexual nature by one inmate, detainee, or resident directed toward another

2. Repeated verbal comments or gestures of a sexual nature to an inmate, detainee, or resident by staff member, contractor, or volunteer, including demeaning references to gender, sexually suggestive or derogatory comments about body or clothing, or obscene language or gestures.

Voyeurism by staff member, contractor, or volunteer means an invasion of privacy of an inmate, detainee, or resident by staff for reasons unrelated to official duties, such as peering at an inmate who is using a toilet in his own cell to perform bodily functions; requiring an inmate to expose his or her buttocks, genitals, or breasts; or taking images of all or part of an inmate's naked body or of an inmate performing bodily functions.

b. Advice from the Federal Bureau of Prisons

This Is How the Bureau Says You Can Prevent Sexual Victimization:

- Carry yourself in a confident manner at all times. (Great Advice!)
- Do not accept gifts or favors from others. (Though you'll probably be okay if someone offers you a care package when you first arrive, mine.)
- Do not accept an offer from another inmate to be your protector. (Avoid anyone who does that, or tell them, point blank, to stay away from you, mine.)
- Be alert. Do not use contraband substances such as drugs or alcohol; these can weaken your ability to stay alert and make good judgments. (Obvious but important.)
- Stay in well-lit areas of the institution (Your homies will point out the areas where the homosexuals rendezvous, with quaint names like *Peter Beach* and *Couple's Corner*. Stay away from them, or you might send out the wrong signals.)
- Choose your associates wisely, look for people who are involved in positive activities like educational programs, psychology groups, or religious services. (If you are on a yard that uses cars, you may get stuck with a group of guys. Pick the most health-conscious ones in the group, and ask them if you can work out with them. Hopefully, some will be involved in other positive activities. If not, pick one or two of the brightest and get them to take a class with you, mine.)
- Find a staff member with whom you feel comfortable discussing your fears and concerns (If you feel suicidal, talk to someone in psychology. Otherwise, avoid staff. They don't want to be your friend, and it will cause problems with other inmates, mine.)
- If you feel fear for your safety, tell a staff member. (If you need protective custody, do this if you are in danger, but try to avoid it if you can. It will create more problems in the long run, mine.)

c. A Final Word on PREA

This law does more than shield prisoners from other inmates. It also grants them safety from staff members. My last few years inside, male correctional officers at Petersburg and Butner were walked off the compounds for sexual relations with inmates. I never heard of a male inmate filing a PREA claim against a female guard, but it may have happened. Any interested women could find hundreds of inmates volunteering for the opportunity, no matter what she looked like, and you can't rape the willing.

Sex is banned in federal prison. Conjugal visits do not exist. One hug and one kiss when partners enter the visiting room, and another when they leave, is all inmates are entitled to by policy. (The pandemic stopped even that for a while.)

Fraternizing with staff will get an inmate sent to the furthest corner of the country. In an instant, they'll find themselves shipped thousands of miles from home. Guys go to the hole for "reckless eyeballing" (staring at a female guard until she feels uncomfortable).

Jackers crowd the higher securities. Their technique is called, "*gunning 'em down*". These perverts hide in the education building or their cells and masturbate while watching a female guard.

One predator in my cellblock at FCI-Beckley ran into our case manager's office and ejaculated on her desk. Then he screamed, "Look what you made me do!" She quit the next day. He caught new charges under PREA.

Consenting homosexuals need to be careful too. I've heard about men having consensual sex and afterwards, one files a PREA claim on the other. Some inmates might do this to get a quick transfer, hurt a boyfriend who cheated, get out of paying a debt, but the biggest motivation is a time cut.

If a *punk* (prison slang: homosexual who plays the female role, usually a prostitute) manages to get a conviction against someone he accuses of rape, there's a chance he can go back to court on a Rule 35(b) and receive a time cut for testifying. Though other inmates have been caught up in the scheme, there is no better target than a homosexual guard.

An inmate performed fellatio on a guard at FCI-Butner. Afterwards, he spit the evidence in a tissue. Then, he approached another guard and claimed he was forced to do the act. The guard was fired and subsequently sentenced to a year in federal prison himself. A similar story took place with another male employee at the FCI-Petersburg facility.

While I was at Petersburg Low, one inmate filed a PREA claim against two men. The "victim" was a prostitute at the prison. Two stories floated around the compound after the incident. The first supported the victim's accusations. The other claimed the "victim" was attempting to get out of paying a large debt.

The FBI locked down that wing of my housing unit. They set up a crime scene and did forensics on the cell. The victim and the two alleged assailants went to the hole. All three were shipped to another prison. I'm not sure of the outcome, but each man faced decades being added to the end of their current sentences.

Cameras cover most of the property at every facility with an exception of bathrooms and cells. So, it would be difficult for another inmate to file a PREA claim against someone they had no interactions with and make it stick. Having said that, be cautious at all times, and if you find yourself a true victim:

- Report your problems to the nearest guard
- Send an email via TRULINCS, or
- Call (or have a local one call) 1-800-656-4673

3. How Much Force Can Staff Use Against Federal Inmates?

Prisons can use force in five situations: self-defense of a third party, enforcement of prison rules and regulations, to prevent escape, and to prevent a crime. Force escalation begins at "reasonable" but raises to "deadly" to prevent a felony. Perimeter trucks carry AR-15s and shotguns with live ammo. They have authorization to shoot anyone attempting escape.

The new penitentiaries are shaped like huge rectangles. The middle is an open space containing the recreation yard. The center has a large gun tower that can cover the entire inner compound. Here, guards can respond quickly to violence with rubber bullets, tear gas, and more.

Federal correctional officers do not carry Billy clubs. When breaking up fights, they tend to tackle participants with overwhelming numbers. They also use judo holds and chokes. They can throw "non-deadly" punches, meaning they have to avoid striking the throat and other vulnerable areas.

It is difficult for a guard to simply attack an inmate and get away with it, but when breaking up a fight or escorting an inebriated prisoner to the hole, things happen. I witnessed a few incidences like this when I first went into custody. An example that stands out in my memory involved two inmates in a fistfight at FCI-Beckley. One knocked the other unconscious. As the scrap ended, guards filled the cellblock yelling. The winner obeyed the commands to lie down on his belly.

The first CO to reach the prone man cuffed his hands behind his back without encountering any resistance, but when the guard finished, the inmate complained that the cuffs were too tight.

The officer screamed, "Shut up!"

Then, he stood up, grabbed the chair between the shackles, and yanked upward viciously. This locked the prone man's arms out straight.

As this was happening, a different CO ran to where the other two were. He jumped into the air and crashed into the convict's elbow with a bent knee. The arm snapped like a tree branch.

My last trip through USP Atlanta's Holdover, I watched a correctional officer handcuff an inmate who disrespected him. After he had the convict secured, he ordered the three other prisoners and myself in the change-out room back into the fishbowl. Before I could exit though, the guard punched the restrained man eight times. He focused on the convict's kidneys and stomach, not wanting to leave visible marks.

Afterwards, the guard offered a choice, "You can rat me out, or you can get on the transfer bus. It'll be your word against mine if you tell. Who do you think they'll believe?"

The convict opted to leave.

When I arrived at USP Yazoo City, a guard openly bragged about a technique he developed. He said he figured out a way to slam "resisting" inmates as he escorted them to the hole and break their collarbones in the process. He may never actually have done this, but he said all he had to do was dump the handcuffed men shoulder-first into the concrete.

Guys in the SHU at FCI-Beckley used to get beat up when they refused to submit to cuffs. When they wouldn't turn backwards, and extend their wrists through the bean flaps to be restrained, it would be considered disobeying a direct order. This defiance authorized several guards to go into the cell and restrain the belligerent inmate. Once they got him bound, they would tune him up.

Stuff like this doesn't happen as much anymore. Now one officer has to carry a camera into the room when they breach a cell. They still make it rough while applying the bracelets, but they have to tone down the extracurricular activity.

Before I went to federal prison, I spent fifteen months in various county jails in North and South Carolina. Throughout that span, it seemed like I got maced every few weeks, and for the most part, I was an innocent bystander each time. After that experience, it seemed strange when I reached my first federal facility, and the guards didn't even carry pepper spray.

They had it on the compound back then, but kept it out of sight. Members of the SERT, the Special Emergency Response Team, were the only ones certified to use it. They only brought it out when they needed it.

That changed in 2015. That year they started a pilot program in certain prisons. At each one, authorized guards started to carry Oleoresin Capsicum: (OC) Aerosol Spray.

Today, every guard carries it. This also caused a decrease in the officer-led violence against inmates. It provides an alternative to fists and allows guards to neutralize unruly individuals from a distance.

Protocol advises them to stand ten to twelve feet away from a noncompliant inmate. They are supposed to spray the face and eyes for two seconds while issuing verbal commands at the same time. If the prisoner doesn't obey within fifteen seconds, they can issue a second burst.

4. Searches

Searches are one of the main tools staff use to reduce violence. They look for hooch and clear, because drunk convicts tend to hurt people, especially guards. They search for weapons to prevent attacks. They try to find contraband phones so shot callers can't put hits on inmates at other prisons. They look for hoarded drugs and stamps, because wealth like this in prison makes certain inmates too powerful. It gives them too much influence.

Inmates have few rights to privacy. Here's a closer look at what to expect:

a. Pat Downs

A guard can frisk you anytime he wants. So can a female. If you don't want a woman touching you, but most guys welcome that, you can ask for a male guard to do it, but don't think it will get you out of the search. They can't touch your crotch, but if they think something is hidden in your underwear, they can demand a strip search.

b. Strip Searches

Usually this is done any time you enter or leave a prison (Self-Surrender, transfer, go to court, or the hospital). It will happen when you leave visitation too. A normal guard will handle it there; however, if a CO on the compound or cellblock wants you to strip, the lieutenant-on-duty will get called over, or you will get sent to the LT's office, for it to take place.

If a guard tries to get you in his office to strip, something is wrong. If he goes in your cell, and tells you to get naked, refuse. Tell him you want to talk to the LT. A weird CO at Petersburg did this to a few guys who ended up filing PREA claims against him. The guard didn't work at the prison much longer after that.

c. Body Searches

These searches take place after fights, brawls, beatdowns, and stabbings whenever they haven't apprehended all the guilty parties. In the cellblock, they will order everyone to go to their rooms, and take off their shirts. At recreation, they will make guys remove shirts and exit in a single file. Staff will lock up (place in the hole) any inmate with cuts, bruises, scratches, rug burn, or banged up knuckles.

d. Cell Searches

1. Random

This happens when the unit guard goes through your cell. Each guard is supposed to hit a few rooms every shift. Usually, cells are chosen at random, but if you do anything to irritate or anger a guard (e.g., get locked out before count, fail inspection with a dirty room, sleep through a standing count, blow off your job) getting your room trashed will be the likely payback.

If the guard takes something, you believe you are entitled to have, ask for a *Confiscation Sheet*. If you can't get it back, you may have to file a *Tort Claim* for compensation. I'll explain this process in detail in Volume III, *Navigating the Federal Bureau of Prison's Rules, Regulations, and Procedures.*

2. Unit Shakedowns

These happen periodically to clear a cellblock for contraband. The laundry staff may hit every room on the compound when they run low on clothing or bed linen. The recreation staff might initiate a shakedown if stuff has been stolen (e.g., ab wheels, jump ropes, yoga mats) SIS may bring drug-sniffing canines through occasionally.

5. Drug and Alcohol Screenings

a. Drug Tests

i. What to Expect

Usually, each facility within the Federal Bureau of Prisons assigns one guard whose sole job is to administer drug tests. USP Yazoo City was the one exception I saw where the lieutenant did it. This thankless task draws a special type man to volunteer for it.

One guard told me he liked my long hair while I had my junk out filling a cup for him. He said it while leaning close enough to feel his breath on my ear. Unsurprisingly, he didn't try to put me in the hole when I finished cursing him out. He would've had some 'splaining to do himself if he dragged me to the lieutenant's office.

Drug screening happens pretty much every day during a normal month at the facility. They only suspend the practice when a lockdown or emergency occurs on the pound. I take that back. I got woken up at 3:00 AM on a Covid quarantine. He passed the cup through the bean flap and meat-gazed through the cell door's window.

With over a thousand inmates at most spots, that's a lot of sausage the stalk. If an inmate gets lucky, this treatment might be years apart. I went through an unfortunate period at Petersburg where they got me six times in as many months. When that happens, all you can do is just grin and bear it (bare it?).

One dirty piss is all it takes to make the *hot list*. If your name hits the list, you have to provide at least one sample every month. That's the best case.

Staff try to trip the hotlist guys. Sometimes back-to back-tests will come a day or a few hours apart. They want to create a false sense of security with the first one and catch users slipping with the second one.

Drug users also have to worry about stool pigeons. If a jailhouse snitch drops a note on another con about getting high, the target might be forced to take multiple tests over a few weeks. Some guys are scandalous inside.

My cellie beat up a guy. In retaliation, the other man dropped a note. As a result, SIS forced my roommate to give eight samples over three weeks. He was clean, but it was still a major hassle. I've even heard of dealers snitching on guys they sold drugs to a few minutes after they got high.

Most institutions use two types of tests. The first give readings in a few minutes. In my experience, they only use them when they catch someone holding drugs and was who was actively wasted. Anyone facing this dilemma fills the cup and crosses fingers for fifteen minutes before he has to pencil a forty-day stay in the box into his itinerary. The second version goes to a lab. They're slower but may be more reliable.

The jars they use get more loving treatment than Little Jimmy's macaroni picture-frame on mom's fridge. You have to wash your hands before you touch it to make sure you haven't dipped your fingers into bleach or another test-cheating chemical. Both you and your bathroom buddy never allow the container to leave your collective sights as you fill it with golden elixir.

With him watching, you seal it with the temper-proof lid. After that, you wrap tape with a unique security code on the lid and bottom. Then, you autograph your creation for posterity and seal it in a mailing package.

ii. New Problems for the Administration Concerning Drugs

These days the tests seem worthless. Prisoners use K-2 and Suboxone, almost exclusively. K-2 has many recipes and different active ingredients. They can't test for them all. In fact, even when inmates have episodes on the drug, they usually don't go to the hole, as long as they never admit to using a drug. The common excuse cons tell medical staff is that they have food poisoning.

Suboxone is an opioid blocker, a modern alternative to methadone. Its chemical makeup prevents normal drug tests from finding it. It's bizarro heroin, the antidote, but it still provides users something close to a pain pill buzz. Cons are cheap dates, because they don't have access to the drug amount they had when they were users on the street. Suboxone hits inmates, down for years, with limited access to smack or fentanyl, much harder than addicts who get it prescribed in the free world.

Why it is so readily available in federal prison? The tab strip it comes in makes it easy to smuggle inside. Also, since it is not an opioid, it carries less legal risk for friends or family members smuggling it to cons who sell it inside.

Regardless of the screening process's effectiveness, FBOP policy allows two hours for providing a sample. No more time is granted to reach the blue line on the cup. Anyone who fails to fill the cup is treated the same as a confirmed user.

The time limit, coupled with the stress the experience creates, causes major problems for guys with shy bladders. Some guards make the experience more grading than necessary. Those petty tyrants will make grown men drop their pants and underwear to their ankles. While doing this, the inmates have to raise their shirts above their bellies the entire time they conduct business. That might've been standard protocol when your mom was teaching you how to keep it in the bowl, but doing it with a closet case blowing stale breath on your neck can start some involuntary clinching in your nether regions.

iii. A Tip for Anyone with a Shy Bladder During Urine Tests

The Bureau gives inmates two hours to produce a sample. Refusal gets treated the same as a failed test. Inmates are allowed to drink a limited amount of water to speed matters, but that is it. I've known more than one man with a shy bladder who ended up in the hole, simply because he couldn't go with an audience watching.

I began practicing yoga and various forms of meditation early in my sentence. It helped me cope with the stress incarceration creates. Here's a simplified technique I always used before giving a sample. It always relaxed me to the point that filling a cup was easy.

As you walk to the testing area, inhale through your nose while mentally counting to five. Exhale through your nose while mentally counting to five. Inhale through your mouth for a count of five. Exhale through your mouth for a count of five. That's one cycle. Start over again. Keep repeating this exercise, over and over, until you finish giving a sample.

Sounds stupid, right? So what? It works.

iv. Sobriety Tests

Guards can make you submit to a breathalyzer test anytime they want. Most assaults on correctional officers happen when angry, frustrated prisoners lose normal inhibitions while drinking. When I first came into the system, staff didn't care about alcohol as long as no one was acting irresponsibly or violently.

Now, blowing dirty or getting caught with alcohol, carries a 100-Series shot. You will be placed on maintenance pay for a year ($5.25 a month no matter the work done). You will lose forty days good time, as well as First Step Time, spend a month or more in the hole, and lose commissary privileges for six months.

Guards usually do random tests during meals. On holidays, they might come into the cellblock for randoms. At some prisons, if you get caught with wine, they will breathalyzer the entire housing unit. This will cause friction with other cars if you cause their homies to go to the hole through your own carelessness.

Blowing dirty or getting caught with alcohol will put you on the *hot list*. This means you will have to provide a urine sample per month for around a year, and you'll be called to the lieutenant's office often to be breathalyzed.

6. MSRA and Other Infectious Diseases

a. Daily Behavior *

*This should not be considered as medical advice. If you have an issue, report to Sick Call and let a qualified medical practitioner diagnose you and offer any potential treatment! *

Unfortunately, if you do a long stretch in a federal correctional facility, you may contract a staph infection or something worse like MSRA. Some prisoners develop a lowered resistance in their skin flora and contract it many times. If you face a short sentence, there are actions you can take to reduce your exposure.

If you want to increase your chances in never contracting the infection, do not scratch itches with your bare fingernails. Use a pen, fork, or scratch the area through clothes or lay a clean rag over the area first. Don't pop zits, pimples, or pick sores. Most importantly, don't stick a finger in your nostrils.

MRSA breeds in nasal pathways. If you get an infection up there, you will battle flareups, for years. Don't go cave diving without a tissue or wash your hands thoroughly first.

Fist bump, or even better, elbow bump the homies to say hello. Covid may already have gotten you away from handshakes, but if not, give them up in prison. Scrub your hands with antibacterial soap after touching any common area item (e.g., remote control, MP3 charging station, ice scoop, thumbprint scanner, or water dispenser).

One of the worst areas is the computers. You have to use a thumbprint scanner to gain access. Some disgusting human beings with dry skin will lick their thumbs before touching the scanner when they have trouble getting it to work. After every email or music/movie download, run to the closest sink.

The phones may be dirtier. I recommend taking a rag and disinfectant spray there with you. If your block has lazy orderlies and a lazier counselor, this might be the only time it gets sanitized. Usually, the mouthpiece smells like the last guy's morning breath.

Some inmates take it a little further. After spraying it down, they use a *phone condom*. They will bring along, a clean, tube sock to the call area and insert the handheld piece into it. Many men make it a habit to use this buffer to escape the funk every time they make a call.

Except for the worst cases, medical usually will not prescribe antibiotics. Instead, they tell inmates to hold hot compresses over the area until a head develops. It might take many hours using a compress, to achieve this. Afterwards, the head gets squeezed until all the blood, pus, and the seed (like a wart but way bigger) gets expelled.

The excretions are highly contagious. If someone else touches it, they could get an infection. Often, inmates touch somewhere else on their body after squeezing and pop a new infection off.

Medical departments lack sympathy in this regard. I had a friend who slid into home base during a softball game. The strawberry on his shin got infected. He went to sick call five times without receiving any treatment. They refused to do anything until his leg tripled in size.

They eventually took him to an outside hospital where a surgeon wanted to amputate. My friend told the doc he would rather die than lose the leg. He got lucky. After two months, and numerous, antibiotics, he survived, but his leg still gives in trouble.

b. Drug Use

First, and hopefully this doesn't need to be said, don't take intravenous drugs. Aside from the normal consequences to becoming a junkie, sterile hypodermic needles are hard to find. Users scrap together a piece of needle, attach something like the barrel from an ink pen, and cap it with rubber to make a *binky*. Addicts get high by sharing these binkies. Besides HIV and Hepatitis C, if an inmate has a MSRA infection, and shares a needle, the highly-resistant staph could honeycomb inside the vein with a high likelihood of death.

c. Tattoos

*Do not consider this to be medical advice. Tattoos are risky behaviors in prison. If you have a medical issue due to them, please go to Sick Call and seek professional help. *

The next risky action inside is getting a tattoo. I got my first MRSA infection from a cellie who didn't clean this fresh ink properly. To make matters worse, he tried to keep his pus-filled arm hidden under long sleeves. He managed to keep me in the dark until I sprouted my own infection, starting with a huge boil on my face.

I battled the infection for a couple months. It took four separate antibiotic scripts to rid my body of the disease. That experience made me borderline OCD when it came to washing my hands and cleaning myself.

If you're considering a tattoo, understand that some staff members write an incident report for any fresh work they see. They don't have to catch you in the act to punish you. For numerous reasons, it will be safer to refrain from getting a tattoo in custody.

If you decide to take the risk anyway, find an artist who practices good hygiene. Purchase your own ink and keep it. Some tattooists try to reuse ink they've spent hours dipping a bloodied needle into, sometimes on different people.

Keep your needle and rig too. Hide it somewhere a guard won't poke his or her finger during a cell search. If that happens, there will be hell to pay. If you end up at a laid-back facility that doesn't sweat tattoos, put your needle in a letter envelope and write, *Tattoo Needle Inside,* on it.

When the artist finishes drilling into you, wash the area with soap and water as hot as you can stand it. I recommend repeating that every couple of hours. Scrub it with antibacterial soap and water at least five times per day until it heals. Once it's clean, some guys put a thin coat of hemorrhoid ointment on it the first day to reduce swelling.

Unless you go to a camp, you won't have access to real ink or anything that shops sell to speed healing and reduce pain. From commissary options, I recommend a thin coat of A&D ointment (diaper rash cream) onto freshly washed skin.

*Don't use the triple antibiotic ointment. *

Neosporin-like cream will pull the cheap, homemade, candle-smut tattoo ink right out of your skin. I had to learn that the hard way. My buddy had to redrill the same tattoo on my back three times before the color stuck.

d. Tuberculosis Skin Tests

Every inmate has to submit to a tuberculosis skin test, PPD, once per year. Refusal can screw up halfway-house placement and transfers to more favorable prisons or programs.

e. Covid

The pandemic locked down the system for two years. It gave extremely lazy staff the opportunity to do even less under the guise of safety. Things have returned to normal for the most part, but expect over-zealous reaction to new strains or diseases: like, enforced mask wearing, extended quarantines, reduced movements, restricted access to recreational equipment, and more.

f. Hepatitis C

This disease is prevalent among drug-addicted inmates. Those infected, and in a progressive state, can receive Harvoni or other treatments which completely cures the disease and would cost many tens of thousands of dollars on the street without insurance.

g. HIV

This is rampant among at risk-inmates. Medical tests if you feel you've been exposed. Sign up at sick call.

In Conclusion

Unfortunately, I can't do anything to prevent your stay at Club Fed, but hopefully, this book has provided enough information to answer your questions, even some you didn't know you had beforehand. One big element of fear and worry is the unknown. Once we have the answers, a big part of those feelings melts away, even when the answers suck.

My goal here was to prepare you for your first months in custody and reassure all those that love you and will miss you while you're away. The next part in my Five Step Process for Preparing Federal Inmates focuses solely on fitting in, adjusting, and staying safe. Check out: *Federal Prison Etiquette: Volume II: New Fish Companion Series.*

http://www.fromcell2soul.com

About the Author

Brooks used meditation, yoga, and Taoist Qigong to survive 23 years in federal prison. His books share his story of how to face terrible hardship and turn the experience into something positive. His works have three objectives to entertain readers with a look at the seldom seen world of federal prison, to help new inmates adjust as quickly as possible, and to help anyone deal with life's difficulties in a more positive way.

About the Publisher

Brooks served twenty-three years in the Federal Bureau of Prisons for a marijuana conspiracy and a 924(C) firearm charge. He survived the sentence by practicing Ashtanga Vinyasa Yoga and Taoist Qigong. Daily meditation helped him cope with the stress of incarceration and put his life on a positive path. It also inspired him to found A Look Inside Personal Growth and Prison Consulting LLC.

This company provides books and audio visual materials to help the newly convicted adjust to prison and quickly and productively as possible. It offers private consulting to pretrial detainees and the families of convicted federal inmates. In addition, the firm offers meditation and Qigong seminars to the public. Our goal is to help our clients live more meaningful lives on both sides of the razor wire.